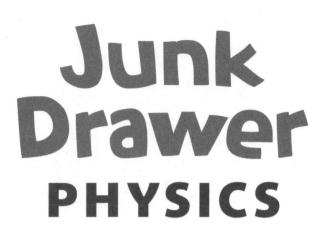

Junk Drawer
PHYSICS

Junk Drawer

PHYSICS

50 AWESOME Experiments | That Don't Cost a Thing

BOBBY MERCER

CHICAGO
REVIEW
PRESS

Published by Chicago Review Press, Incorporated
814 North Franklin Street
Chicago, Illinois 60610

ISBN 978-1-61374-920-3

Library of Congress Cataloging-in-Publication Data
Mercer, Bobby, 1961- author.
   Junk drawer physics : 50 awesome experiments that don't cost a thing / Bobby Mercer. —
First edition.
      pages cm
   Audience: 9+
   ISBN 978-1-61374-920-3 (trade paper)
   1. Physics—Experiments—Juvenile literature. I. Title.
      QC25.M35 2014
      530.078—dc23
                                                                    2013046726

Cover design and art: Andrew Brozyna, AJB Design, Inc.
Interior design: Rattray Design

Printed in the United States of America
5 4 3 2 1

To Jordan and Nicole, I hope you always enjoy the wonder of why.

Contents

Acknowledgments

B ooks don't happen without great people. Thanks to all the people who helped turn the idea for *Junk Drawer Physics* into this book: Kathy Green for being a great agent. Jerome Pohlen, Amelia Estrich, and the creative people at Chicago Review Press for making it look great. Thanks to my wonderful family. Michele, you are amazing and understanding when I don't put the glue back. Nicole, for helping me build most of the activities this book. Jordan, thanks for making us all smile. A special thanks to Team Science: Jennifer Allsbrook, Shannon Haynes, Kim Mirasola, Laura Spinks, and Sergey Zalevskiy.

Introduction

We all have a junk drawer containing the odds and ends that we accumulate as we go through life. In the pages of this book, you will find out that all that junk can help teach you science. The fun projects in this book will use inexpensive or no-cost objects. Most of it is stuff you probably already have.

Hands-on science is entertaining for everybody—fun for kids from 5 to 85. Enjoy yourself, be careful, and you just might learn something.

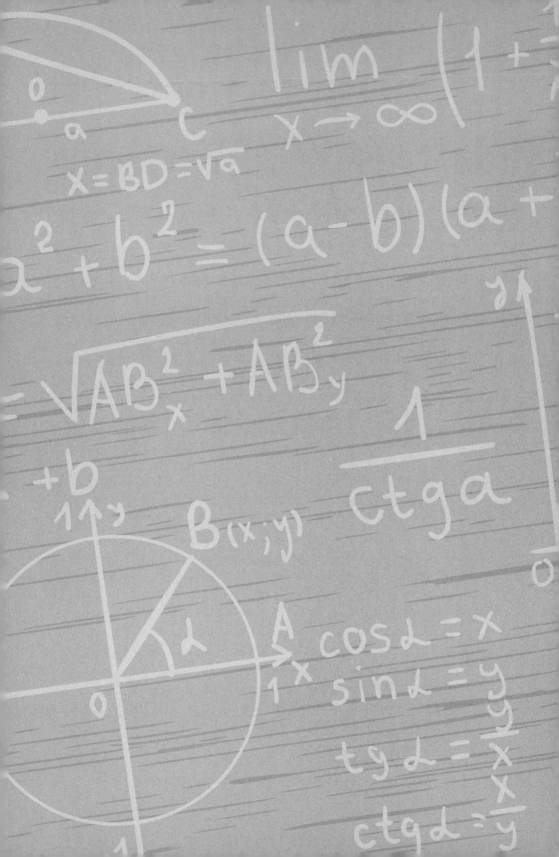

$$\lim_{x \to \infty} \left(1 + \frac{1}{x}\right)$$

$$x = BD = \sqrt{a}$$

$$a^2 + b^2 = (a - b)(a +$$

$$= \sqrt{AB^2_x + AB^2_y}$$

$$\frac{1}{ctg\alpha}$$

$$B(x;y)$$

$$\alpha$$

$$\cos\alpha = x$$
$$\sin\alpha = y$$
$$tg\alpha = \frac{y}{x}$$
$$ctg\alpha = \frac{x}{y}$$

1

Forces and Motion

Mesmerizing CD Top

Turn an old CD into a mind-bending tabletop spinner. Spin, stare, and watch the world change.

Adult supervision required

From the Junk Drawer:

☐ Old CD
☐ Paper
☐ Markers

☐ Scissors
☐ Superglue or hot glue
☐ 2 flat glass beads

Step 1: Trace around a CD on a piece of paper. Use a marker to create swirls going out from the center, as shown. Then cut around the outside of the CD line.

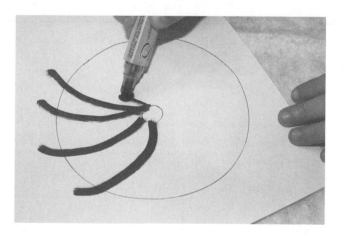

Step 2: You need adult permission or help for this step. Lay a piece of scrap paper on your work surface to catch any glue that drips. Use hot glue or superglue to affix the round piece of paper to the CD. Then glue one glass bead to each side of the hole in the center of the CD, with the flat sides facing the hole. These glass beads are commonly found in craft stores and are used as decorations for flower vases, tabletop water fountains, and candle sets. Let the glue dry completely.

Step 3: If you color in the swirls, it will make them wider, which will make the illusion better.

Step 4: Pinch the top glass bead with your fingers and spin it. Practice until you can get it to spin like a top while sitting in place.

Step 5: Now spin the top and lean directly over it. Stare at the center for about 30 seconds as it spins, then look up at a plain wall. It should make the wall spin a little bit. Keep practicing until you master it.

Try staring at the top for different amounts of time. Crazy! Do it again and look at other things. Amaze your friends as you warp the world around you. You can make other tops and try different patterns and colors.

The Science Behind It

The spiral on the top of the CD "trains" your eyes to follow the swirl. This effect is called *persistence of vision.* Your brain holds onto an image for a fraction of a second. Since that image is a spinning spiral, when you look at a wall or something else, it will spiral for a few seconds. It might take a few tries to get good at it. (Even if you don't always get the swirl effect, you still made a fun top.)

Grocery List Tug-of-War

Use a piece of paper to learn about inertia.

From the Junk Drawer:

☐ Several strips of paper   ☐ Coins
☐ Scissors   ☐ Tape

Step 1: For this experiment, you need several strips of paper. A long grocery
list notepad will work, or you can take a sheet of letter size paper and
cut it into four strips. Paper that is already written on is perfect—you're
recycling.

  In each strip, make two cuts that almost go through the paper, as
shown. To do this, fold each strip of paper, but do not crease the center.
This will insure the cuts are equal in length.

Step 2: Pick up a single strip, holding one end in each hand. Your goal is to
try to tear both ends off at the same time so that you are left with just the

center part. First, pull slowly and watch what happens. Then repeat with another strip and try pulling faster. Can you do it?

Step 3: Now tape four or five coins to the center section of a cut strip.

Step 4: Quickly pull on the ends of the strip and watch what happens this time. The trick is to pull fast and hard.

The Science Behind It

Inertia is the tendency of an object to resist changes in motion. A heavy object is hard to start moving, but a heavy object is also harder to stop once it is moving. Just think of a semitruck on the interstate and how long it takes to come to a stop.

When you try this experiment with paper alone, the center piece doesn't have much inertia—it's light. When you tug it, one end tears before the other, leaving two pieces together. But when you tape coins to the center section, you give that section extra inertia. This time, when you tug quickly, the center section wants to stay in place more than before (it has more inertia). The ends tear off, leaving you with just the center.

Jar Spin

Defy gravity as you take a ball for a spin.

From the Junk Drawer:

☐ Clear, large-mouth plastic jar   ☐ Small bouncy ball
   (mayonnaise or peanut butter jars
   work well) with label removed

Step 1: Place a clear plastic jar mouth-down over a small bouncy ball.
   (Don't do this on a nice wooden table.) Ping-pong balls also work well.

Step 2: Grasp the bottom of the jar. While keeping the jar's mouth on
   the table, swirl the jar quickly in small circles, causing the ball to roll in
   circles as well. Move the jar faster, until you can pick up both the jar and
   the ball.

The Science Behind It

As you swirl the jar in a circle, the ball wants to move in a straight line. Of course, it can't, because the jar is in the way. The jar supplies a **centripetal** (center-seeking) *force* on the ball. The ball pushes back against this centripetal force, which creates **friction** between the inside of the jar and the ball. When the speed of the ball is great enough, the friction will keep the it "glued" to the inside wall as you lift the jar.

Floating Coin

Magically lift a coin with science.

From the Junk Drawer:

☐ Crisp dollar bill (or piece of paper)   ☐ Coin

Step 1: Fold a dollar bill in half so it forms a *V*, as shown. You can also do
this with a stiff piece of paper. Place the coin over the *V*.

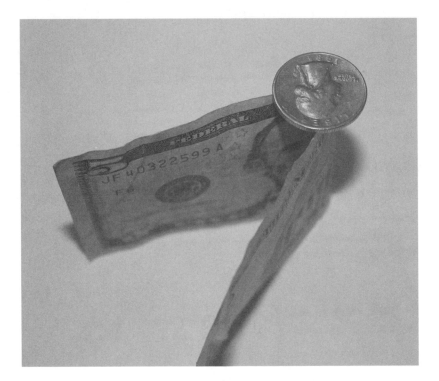

Step 2: Slowly pull apart the two ends of the dollar bill. The coin should stay
in place and balance on the paper. Now slowly lift the dollar bill, picking
up the coin with it. With practice and a steady hand, you can pick up the
coin even when the bill is completely straight. Practice this trick, then
amaze your parents, friends, and teachers.

The Science Behind It

All objects have a *center of mass*. If the center of mass is over a support, the object will stay balanced. When you balance on one foot, you have to move your center of mass over that foot. Try it; as you lift one foot up, your body will naturally move your center of mass over the other foot. Similarly, when you slowly pull the ends of the dollar bill, the center of mass for the coin will move directly over the dollar bill. As long as the center of mass stays over the supporting object, you can pick up the coin.

Crash Test Dummy

Learn Newton's laws with a dummy to help.

From the Junk Drawer:

☐ Toy car   ☐ Rubber band
☐ Small action figure   ☐ Large marshmallow

Step 1: Set a crash test dummy—a plastic action figure—on a toy car. Push the toy car into a wall. What happens to the dummy?

Step 2: Put the crash test dummy back on the car. This time, use a rubber band to attach the dummy to the roof. Make sure the rubber band does not interfere with the wheels. Push the toy car into a wall again. What happens?

Step 3: Put the action figure on the car one last time. Use a rubber band seat belt, but add a large marshmallow to act as an airbag. Now run your crash test dummy into the wall again.

The Science Behind It

Isaac Newton was a man of incredible genius. He studied motion, **gravity**, **energy**, light, math, and chemistry. His three laws of motion serve as the cornerstone of modern day physics. This Crash Test Dummy experiment can teach you about his *first law of motion*.

Newton's first law of motion states that a body at rest will stay at rest and a body in motion will stay in motion, unless acted upon by an unbalanced force. When the car runs into the wall in Step 1, your action figure keeps going. When the dummy finally hits the wall, it encounters an unbalanced force, and it stops. Ouch! In Step 2, the rubber band (seat belt) provides the unbalanced force and the figure stops with the car.

When you wear a seatbelt in a car, the seatbelt stops you when the car stops during normal driving. An airbag will further help your body stop in a car crash, though your car's airbag does not taste like a marshmallow. Seat belts and airbags have saved countless lives over the years.

At 50 miles per hour, one-half of the energy from the burning gasoline in a car is used to overcome air resistance.

Rolling Uphill

Use two funnels to create another design that defies gravity.

From the Junk Drawer:

☐ 2 small funnels

☐ Tape

☐ 2 wooden boards

☐ A few books

Step 1: Place two funnels together with the large openings facing each other, then tape them together as shown.

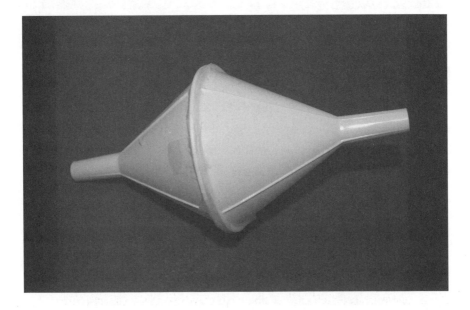

Step 2: Stand two boards on their narrow edges. Place one end of each board on a book. One thick book is probably enough, or use several small books. Push the other two ends together so that the boards make a *V*. The wide part of the *V* should be equal to the width of the wide part of the two funnels.

Step 3: Place the two-funnel piece at the narrow part of the *V* and watch it roll uphill. You may need to experiment to get the height or angle of the boards just right. The picture is taken from above to help you see how to place the boards and funnel. After you have perfected the setup, share it with your friends, parents, and teacher. The activity is better viewed from the side, as this allows you to really see the funnels roll uphill.

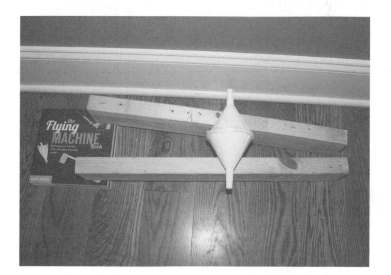

The Science Behind It

The funnels have a *center of gravity* directly between the two wide openings of the funnels. The center of gravity is the point at which all **mass** is centered. When the funnels roll, the center of gravity is actually going down, as is expected. But the funnels' shape allows you to see the optical illusion of the funnels rolling uphill, even though the center of gravity actually rolls downhill.

Cork Accelerometer

Learn about acceleration with an old cork.

Adult supervision required

From the Junk Drawer:

☐ Cork   ☐ Hot glue gun
☐ Scissors   ☐ Empty clear plastic bottle with lid
☐ String   ☐ Water

Step 1: Get assistance from an adult for the first three steps. First, use the point of a pair of scissors to create a small hole in the top of a cork that is small enough to fit inside your plastic bottle.

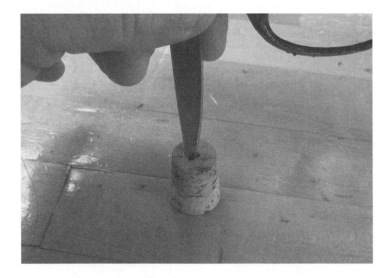

Step 2: Cut a piece of string slightly shorter than your empty plastic bottle. With adult help, use the hot glue gun to glue one end of the string into the hole in the cork.

Step 3: With adult help, use the hot glue gun to glue the other end of the string to the center of the inside of the bottle's lid. Let the glue dry completely.

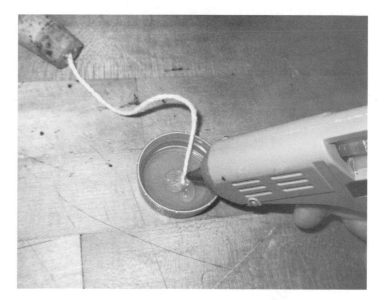

Step 4: Take the wrapper off the clear plastic bottle. Fill the bottle with water. Leave less than ½ inch of air at the top.

Step 5: Do this step in the sink or on a surface that can get wet. Push the cork inside the bottle. Tightly screw on the lid (with the attached string). It is OK if some air is in the bottle.

Step 6: Turn the Cork Accelerometer upside down. Now walk around with the Cork Accelerometer. Hold it in front of you and pay attention to the cork. Take the Cork Accelerometer on your next car or bus ride. The cork will show you the direction of the acceleration. Did you see any movements that surprised you?

The Science Behind It

You are familiar with speedometers in cars—they measure speed. Accelerometers measure **acceleration**, the change in speed, although this accelerometer only gives you the direction of the acceleration. Objects accelerate whenever they experience an unbalanced force.

When you sit still, the forces on your body are equal. To accelerate, you need an extra unbalanced force. Pushing with your feet to start moving provides an unbalanced force. This unbalanced force gives you an acceleration that you can see with the cork. As you speed up, the cork goes forward. Positive acceleration is when you speed up.

When you are walking at a constant speed in a straight line, the cork will stay right in the middle of the water. You have zero acceleration, even though you are moving. Constant speed in a straight line means you have no unbalanced force. And no unbalanced force means zero acceleration.

You slow down because an unbalanced force acts against you. This is called *deceleration*. When you slow down, the cork will move in the direction opposite of the one in which you are moving. The cork shows you the direction of the unbalanced force (and the acceleration).

In the Cork Accelerometer, water also plays a valuable role. Water is denser than the cork. So a cork-sized amount of water has more mass. More mass equals more inertia, so the water wants to keep moving in the same direction it was originally. Since the water surrounds the cork, it provides a **buoyant** force that pushes on the cork and shows the direction of the unbalanced force. When you speed up, the water wants to stay still, so more water moves to the back of the jar, which pushes the cork forward (showing positive acceleration). As you slow down, the water wants to keep moving; more water moves to the front of the jar, which pushes the cork back (showing negative acceleration).

Accelerometers are commonly used inside game controllers and smartphones. These accelerometers don't use water and a cork, but tiny chips made of **silicon**. By creating three tiny silicon accelerometers, they can tell up from down and sideways. These accelerometers are what tell the screen to flip on your smartphone. A similar device feels the acceleration in your game controller and sends commands to the gaming system.

Speeding up and slowing down takes an unbalanced force. So does turning a corner, but more on that in our next *Junk Drawer Physics* contraption.

Spinning Force Machine

Learn centripetal force with this homemade spinner.

Adult supervision required

From the Junk Drawer:

☐ String

☐ 2 fishing bobbers or corks

☐ Hot glue

☐ 2 empty plastic jars (mayonnaise or peanut butter jars work well) with lids

☐ Water

☐ Old paint stirrer or ruler

☐ Lazy Susan (turntable)

☐ Towel

Step 1: Use two pieces of string that are slightly shorter than the overall height of your jars. Tie the first piece of string to a fishing bobber or have an adult help you use hot glue to attach the string to a cork. You can use any two small floating objects. Now repeat for the other object with the second piece of string.

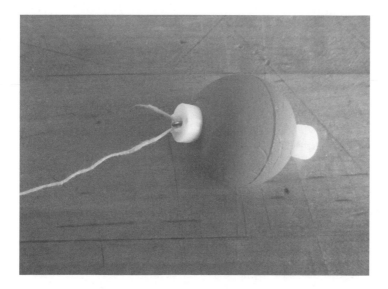

Step 2: Hot glue the free end of each string to the center of the inside of your jar lids. Let the hot glue dry before you go on to the next step. Always get adult help or permission to use a hot glue gun.

Step 3: Do this next step over a sink to save yourself some cleanup. Fill the jars completely full of water. Fill them until they start to overflow. Now push one cork or bobber into the water in each jar and tighten the lids. Turn the jars upside-down over the sink and check for leaks. Get an adult or older sibling to tighten the jar lids if they leak. Dry off the outside of the jars completely.

Step 4: Glue or tape a paint stirrer or ruler across the middle of a lazy Susan. You could also use a spinning office chair or an old record player if you have one, but skip the glue. I recommend paint stirrers, since most of us have several around the house, but an old ruler will also work. Hardware stores will give you a paint stirrer if you don't have one at home.

Step 5: Using hot glue, attach the jar lids to either end of the old ruler or paint stirrer. The jars should be upside-down. Allow the glue to cool completely.

Step 6: Before you spin the lazy Susan, which way do you think the bobbers will move? Now spin the turntable and watch the bobbers. Experiment with different speeds.

The Science Behind It

Objects naturally move in a straight line. For an object to curve, an unbalanced force must be applied. This unbalanced force is called **centripetal force**. It is always directed toward the center of a circle. The bobbers are free to move in any direction, but they go to the inside of the circle because of the centripetal force.

As the turntable spins faster, the bobbers lean more toward the center, since this centripetal force depends more on the speed than any other factor. The amount of force also depends upon the **radius** of the curve and the mass of the bobbers, but we didn't change those in this experiment. You could devise experiments to test those if you wanted to.

Water also plays a role in showing this centripetal force. The water and bobbers both want to keep moving in a straight line. Since the water is denser than the floating objects, it does a better job of moving straight, so water is pushed to the outside of the jars. More water outside the bobbers provides a buoyant force that pushes the bobber toward the center of the circle. The water helps to show you the direction of the centripetal force.

When you ride in a car (or amusement ride) that turns a corner sharply, you feel something slightly different. You feel your body being pushed outward. That is because your body wants to continue in a straight line, but the car supplies an inward centripetal force through the seat and seat belts. Newton's third law of motion states that for every action there is an equal and opposite reaction. What you feel is a force equal to the car's centripetal force. But the force you feel is opposite in direction. Hence, our body senses an outward force.

Isaac Newton was born on Christmas day.

Paper Drop

Repeat Galileo Galilei's famous experiment in your own house.

From the Junk Drawer:

☐ Scrap piece of paper

☐ Any unbreakable object heavier than the paper

Step 1: You need a piece of paper out of the recycling bin and some object that is OK to drop. Balls, pens, and key rings will all work. Just make sure that whatever you select is unbreakable. Hold both objects at eye level and drop. The heavier object hits the ground first. Why?

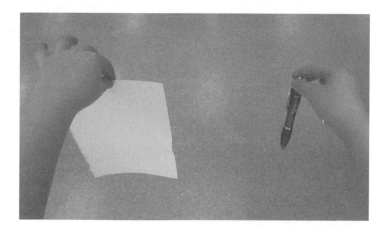

Step 2: Now crumple the paper into the tiniest ball possible. Hold both objects at eye level and drop again. Now they hit the ground at the same time. Why? Throw the crumpled up piece of paper back in the recycling bin.

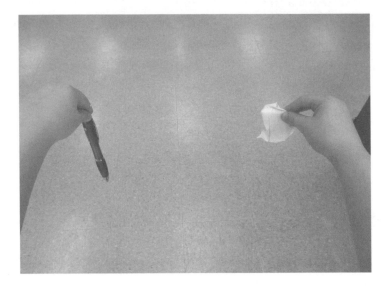

The Science Behind It

Galileo reportedly performed almost the same experiment over 500 years ago from the Leaning Tower of Pisa. He selected two cannonballs of different materials and different weights. He then dropped them from the tower and they hit the ground at the same time. This led him to the conclusion that heavier objects accelerate toward earth at the same rate that light objects do, in the absence of air.

When you dropped the paper in Step 1, it took more time because it had more **air resistance**. By crumpling up the paper, you eliminated much of the air resistance. Without air resistance, all falling objects accelerate at the same rate.

In 1971, astronaut David Scott performed the same experiment on the Moon. The Moon has gravity (but less than Earth) but no air. Scott dropped a hammer and a feather and they hit the ground at the same time. You just did almost the same experiment, but you didn't have to go to Italy or the Moon.

Galileo's middle finger is on display in the Museo Galileo in Florence, Italy. The finger was removed when Galileo's body was reburied in 1737. The rest of his body is buried elsewhere in Florence.

Weightless Cup

Be an astronaut . . . or at least demonstrate what they feel. This is a great activity to do outside when the weather is nice. You can do it inside if you get permission.

From the Junk Drawer:

☐ Paper clip

☐ Old paper or Styrofoam cup

☐ Water

☐ Video recorder (optional)

Step 1: Straighten part of a paper clip by folding out one leg. Poke two holes in your cup on opposite sides, about 1 inch above the bottom.

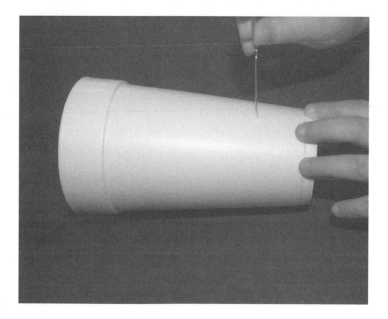

Step 2: If you're indoors, do this step over a sink. Put your fingers over the holes and fill the cup with water. While holding the cup, remove your fingers and watch the water come out of the holes.

Step 3: Refill the cup again with your fingers over the holes. Hold it up in the air as high as possible. Drop the cup and observe whether water comes out of the holes as it falls. No water will come out of the holes! Fill it up again and repeat.

Optional Step 4: You can have a friend help (or use a tripod) to film the fall. This is a great option, since it is hard to see the cup as it quickly falls. Even a cell phone video camera has strong enough resolution to prove that water doesn't come out as the cup falls.

The Science Behind It

Gravity causes all objects to fall. As you learned in the Paper Drop (page 25), all objects accelerate at the same rate if air resistance is about the same. In Step 2, gravity causes the water to fall, and it runs out of the holes. But in Step 3, the water doesn't run out of the holes because the water and the cup are falling together. The water is accelerating and the cup is also accelerating. Since both the cup and the water accelerate at the same rate, the water stays in the cup. In a sense, the water feels "weightless."

You may have felt weightless for very short periods of time in your life. If you have ever been in a car driving over a railroad track really fast, you may have felt it. You may have felt it going down the drop hill on a roller coaster. Or a Drop Zone ride at the fair. A Drop Zone ride picks you up and then drops you in **free fall**. Since you and your seat are falling at the same rate, your butt doesn't press on the seat and you feel weightless for a second or two.

The astronauts on the NASA International Space Station (ISS) feel weightless the entire time they are in space. Astronauts train for years before they go into space to get used to the feeling of weightlessness. Believe it or not, the ISS is falling down toward the Earth, but it is also moving so fast in the horizontal direction, out into space, that it "misses" the Earth. And since both the astronauts and the ISS are falling at the same rate, the astronauts feel weightless, just like the water in the Weightless Cup.

Astronauts in orbit are not weightless. Their weight provides the centripetal force that keeps them in orbit. They are falling, but they are moving so fast sideways that they stay the same distance above the Earth's surface. The speed needed to orbit depends on the desired orbit height. The first person to write about this was Isaac Newton, who said that the Moon was falling and actually proved it!

See-Saw Candles

Create a fun, flaming see-saw.

Adult supervision required

From the Junk Drawer:

☐ Drinking straw   ☐ 2 birthday candles

☐ Scissors   ☐ Tape

☐ Ruler   ☐ 2 drinking glasses (or soup

☐ Sewing needle (or straight pin)   cans)

☐ Toothpick or paper clip   ☐ Match

Step 1: If using a flexible straw, cut off the flexible end. Using your
   ruler, measure the exact length of the straw and divide that length by
   two. Push a needle through the straw at the exact center. Slide a
   toothpick or a straightened paper clip through the hole in both sides
   of the straw.

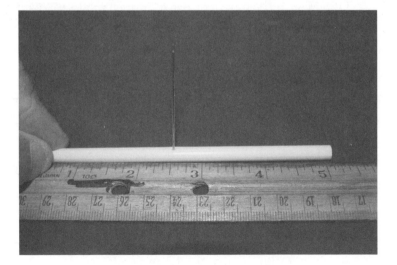

Step 2: Slide one birthday candle into each end of the straw, inserting the same length on both ends, but leaving most of the candles sticking out of the straw. Secure the candles by wrapping a small piece of tape around each one.

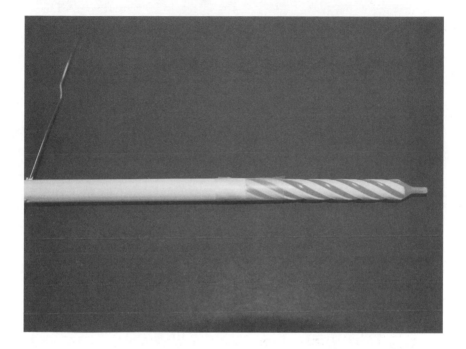

Step 3: The straw should balance in the middle, since you have equal weight on both sides of the needle. The experiment will still work even if it is off by a tiny bit. But if it is *way* off, move the candles into or out of the straw until it balances. Then place two drinking glasses (or soup cans) upside-down about 1 inch apart—these will be your supports, so make sure they are not flammable. Balance the See-Saw Candle between the two supports by resting the paper clip on the upside-down glasses.

Warning: wax will drip from both candles during this experiment, so do this activity on countertops that clean easily. Use a kitchen

counter or bathroom counter if the countertop is granite or marble.
You can use an aluminum pie pan or large baking tray if you are worried
about the countertop.

Step 4: Now you're ready to light the candles. Always get adult permission to
use fire. Using a match, light the candle on the lowest end first. Now light the
candle on the other end and watch the straw start to see-saw. Clean up the
wax on your flat surface when you are done. Because it is so cool, this is a junk
drawer science trick that needs to be shared with parents, teachers, and friends.

The Science Behind It

The See-Saw Candle is balanced initially because the weight on both sides of the needle is the same. As one side burns up wax, it will lose weight. As it loses weight, it will rise, since it is now lighter. Both ends will take turns as the heavier side. The See-Saw Candle will work until the flames go out.

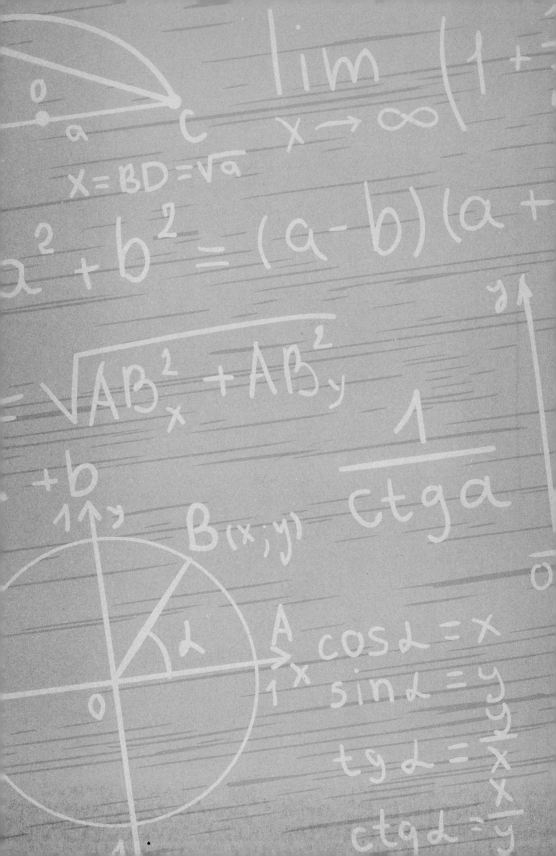

$$\lim_{x \to \infty} \left(1 + \right.$$

$$O$$
$$a$$
$$C$$

$$x = BD = \sqrt{a}$$

$$a^2 + b^2 = (a - b)(a +$$

$$= \sqrt{AB_x^2 + AB_y^2}$$

$$+b$$

$$B(x,y)$$

$$\frac{1}{ctg\alpha}$$

$$\alpha$$
$$A$$
$$O$$

$$\cos\alpha = x$$
$$\sin\alpha = y$$
$$tg\alpha = \frac{y}{x}$$
$$ctg\alpha = \frac{x}{y}$$

Energy

Balloon Shooter

Turn a drink bottle into an entertaining little launcher.

Adult supervision required

From the Junk Drawer:

- ☐ Empty drink bottle (plastic)
- ☐ Scissors
- ☐ Balloon
- ☐ Tape
- ☐ Projectiles (soft and safe)

Step 1: First, make sure you get adult help or permission, and then use scissors or a sharp knife to cut off the neck of an empty plastic bottle. Make sure to recycle the remaining part of the bottle.

    Note to teachers and homeschool parents: You can start the cuts in many bottles with a sharp knife, then let your students finish the cut with any type of safety scissors.

Step 2: Cut the neck off a balloon and discard the neck part. Stretch the opening of the balloon over the entire neck piece of the bottle.

Step 3: Use a small strip of tape to secure the balloon to the bottle. The picture shows masking tape, but any tape will work. The balloon shooter will actually work without *any* tape if you don't pull too hard.

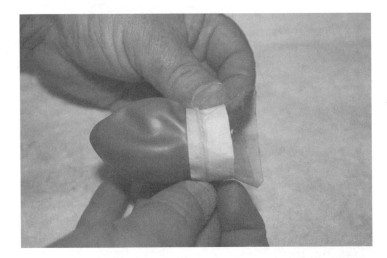

Step 4: Load your launcher by inserting your projectile into the balloon. Good safe types of projectiles are small balls of paper, raisins, balls of tape, and gumballs. The launcher will fire anything that fits through the neck of the plastic bottle.

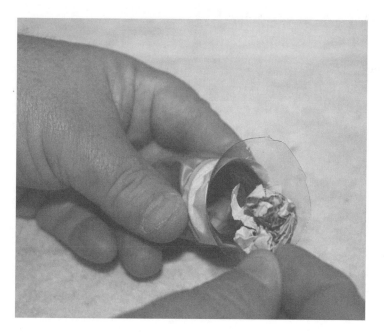

Step 5: While holding on to the bottle neck with one hand, pull back the balloon with your other hand and let it fly. Make sure you aim away from friends, parents, brothers, sisters, pets, and breakable stuff.

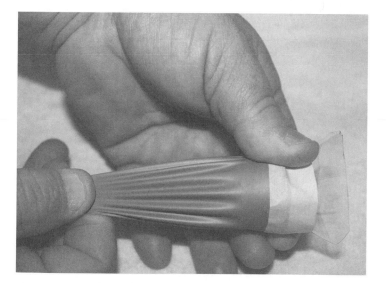

The Science Behind It

When you pull on the balloon, the rubber in the balloon stores elastic *potential energy*. When you let go of the balloon, the rubber in the balloon snaps back to its original shape. Most of the elastic energy is converted into *kinetic energy*, which is transferred to the projectile. Since kinetic energy is energy of motion, so your projectile flies across the room.

Clothespin Catapult

Launch "cannonballs" across the room with this miniature catapult.

Adult supervision required

From the Junk Drawer:

☐ Clothespin
☐ Plastic spoon
☐ Hot glue

☐ Scrap of wood (about 4 inches long)
☐ Cannonball

Step 1: Get adult help or permission to use hot glue gun. Hot glue one side of a clothespin to a scrap of wood as shown. Allow it to cool. With hot glue, it will only take about two minutes to dry.

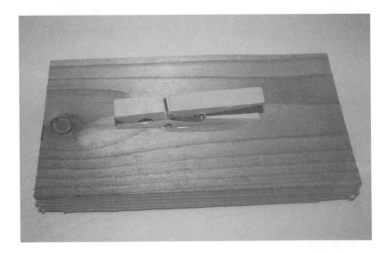

Step 2: Hot glue the spoon to the top half of the clothespin. The bowl of the spoon should be facing up. Let it cool completely.

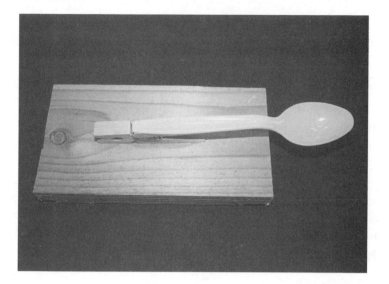

Step 3: Hold the scrap of wood in one hand. Load your "cannonball" (balls of paper, grapes, small bouncy balls, ping-pong balls, and marshmallows all make great, safe cannonballs) into the bowl of the spoon with the other hand. Then use your fingertips to pull down the tip of the spoon and let it fly. Aim away from people, pets, and breakable stuff.

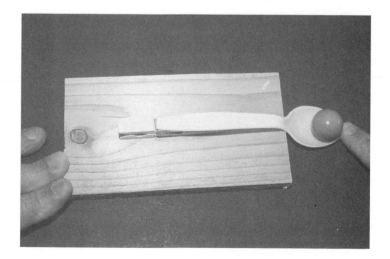

The Science Behind It

All catapults work because of elastic potential energy. When you bend something that is elastic, it wants to return to its original shape. The clothespin works because of the tiny, metal piece (it is actually a spring) at the center. When squeezed and released, this metal piece will cause the clothespin to spring back. But the Clothespin Catapult gets a double boost of elastic potential energy from the spoon. When bent a little, plastic will also spring back. Be careful though; if you bend a plastic spoon too far, it will break.

Door-to-Door Launcher

Use a doorstop to create a fun catapult.

From the Junk Drawer:

☐ Spring-style doorstop   ☐ Plastic spoon
☐ Duct tape   ☐ Projectiles

Step 1: Wrap a piece of duct tape around the screw end of a spring-style doorstop for safety.

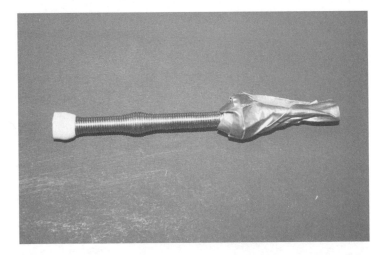

Step 2: Duct tape a plastic spoon to the doorstop. You want the end of the plastic spoon about in the middle of the doorstop. This is your Door-to-Door Launcher.

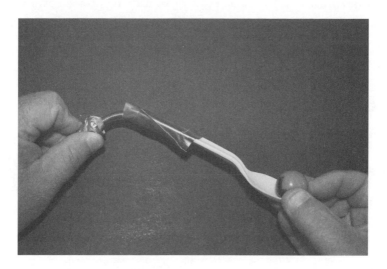

Step 3: Hold the bottom of the Door-to-Door Launcher in one hand. Load up the spoon with projectiles and pull back with the other hand. Marshmallows, grapes, bouncy balls, and acorns all make great, safe projectiles. Aim away from people, pets, and breakable stuff.

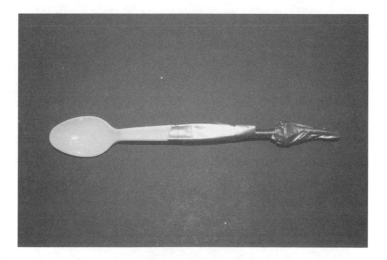

The Science Behind It

As with the Clothespin Catapult, you are converting the elastic potential energy of the spring into kinetic energy for your flying projectiles. You get a double dose of elastic potential energy from the bending of the spoon and the bending of the doorstop spring. More energy equals more fun!

Ball Blaster

Send a ball screaming to the roof with this unique creation.

Adult supervision required

From the Junk Drawer:

- ☐ At least three different size bouncy balls
- ☐ Drill and bits
- ☐ Vice
- ☐ Wooden skewer
- ☐ Superglue

- ☐ Ruler
- ☐ Pen or pencil
- ☐ Scissors
- ☐ Sandpaper (optional)
- ☐ Clear tape
- ☐ Safety goggles

Step 1: Adult help is needed for the first few steps. Select a drill bit that is the exact size as the wooden skewer. Put the largest bouncy ball in a vice. Drill a hole about halfway through the bouncy ball. If a vice is not available, you could tape the ball to a scrap of wood using duct tape. For safety purposes, **never** attempt to hold something in your hand as you drill.

Step 2: With adult help, squeeze some superglue into the hole and slide in the wooden skewer. Set this aside so the glue can dry.

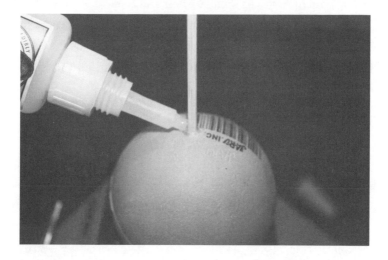

Step 3: Put the second largest bouncy ball in the vice. Select the next size drill bit. The drill bit should be slightly larger than the wooden skewer for this ball. Drill a hole all the way through this ball. If you have more than three balls, repeat Step 3 for all the bouncy balls *except* the smallest one. Finally, put the smallest bouncy ball in the vice. Select a drill bit that is much larger than the wooden skewer; ¼-inch should work well. Drill a hole all the way through this ball.

Step 4: Hold the largest bouncy ball and wooden skewer on a table. Stack all the balls from smallest to largest, sliding them over the skewer. Use a ruler to measure 1-inch above the smallest ball and make a mark with a pen or pencil. Remove the top ball. With scissors, cut the skewer at the mark. If the scissors won't cut the skewer, cut as far as you can and then snap it with your hands. You might want to use sandpaper to smooth the end.

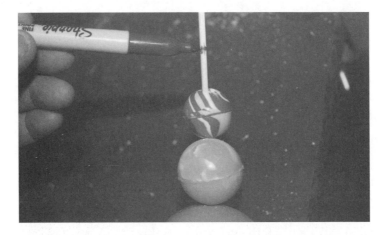

Step 5: Wrap a piece of clear tape around the skewer where the smallest bouncy ball would normally be. The small ball should slide freely off this tape, but the middle balls should not be able to slide over the tape. (Drill the hole in the smallest ball larger if you need to.) Put the small ball over the tape, and if it slides freely, get ready to blast off. Note: you can skip the tape if you want to, but all the balls may bounce in crazy directions.

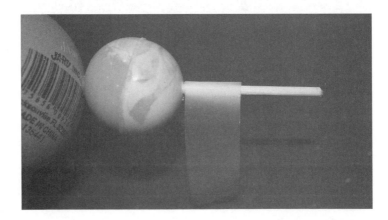

Step 6: You need to do this last step outside or in a room with no breakable items. You also need to do it on a hard surface such as a driveway or a wood or tile floor. Put on a pair of sunglasses or safety goggles. Hold the top of the wooden skewer at eye level, with the largest ball hanging down. Look up into the air while letting the Ball Blaster fall to the floor. When it hits the ground, the top ball should blast off from the wooden skewer. Go find the ball and do it again. Amaze your parents, friends, and teacher with your junk drawer Ball Blaster.

The Science Behind It

The Ball Blaster is a great demonstration of **momentum** and **energy**. Energy is the ability to move things, and momentum is a measure of mass and speed. When you hold the Ball Blaster in the air, it has potential (stored) energy. As the entire Ball Blaster falls, the potential energy is changed into kinetic (action) energy. When the large ball hits the ground, its kinetic energy changes direction from down to up. The energy is transferred through the balls to the top ball, and it leaves at super speed. But first you need to know about momentum to completely understand what is going on.

Momentum is a measure of motion, and it depends upon mass and speed. A bowling ball has more momentum than a soccer ball if they roll at the same speed because of its higher mass. But a soccer ball could have more momentum if it were moving very fast. When the large bouncy ball hits the ground, its momentum (and energy) is transferred into the next ball up, like what happens when balls on a pool table hit each other. It will gain all of the momentum from the big ball. And since the next ball is smaller (in mass), it will move at a higher speed to maintain the same momentum. The momentum is transferred again to the next smaller ball, which will move even faster. The smallest ball will then slide off the tape with super speed because it has all the momentum from the larger balls. And less mass equals more speed.

Quick Freeze Ice

Watch ice form in a matter of seconds.

From the Junk Drawer:

- ☐ Plastic bottles of purified or distilled water
- ☐ Cooler
- ☐ Ice
- ☐ Salt
- ☐ Water
- ☐ Ceramic plate or cooking pan

Step 1: Put several drinking-sized bottles of purified or distilled water in a cooler. Fill the cooler about halfway with ice. Make sure the bottles are completely surrounded by the ice. Add about ¼ cup of salt to the top of the ice. Ice cream salt, rock salt, or table salt will all work.

Step 2: Finish filling the cooler with ice all the way up to the necks of the bottles. Then add some more salt to the top layer of ice. Pour two cups of water into the cooler to help melt some of the ice. Leave the cooler alone for at least 15 minutes so the water can get really cold. But do not bump or move the table the cooler is on while the bottles chill in the salty ice water mix.

Step 3: Place a small piece of clean, unsalted ice in the middle of a ceramic plate (or metal cooking pan). Remove one of the bottles from the salty ice water mix and unscrew the top. Immediately begin to pour a tiny stream of water onto the piece of ice on the plate.

Step 4: Continue to pour a small stream of water onto the ice, and watch as a column of ice grows upward. See how high you can get the ice **stalagmite**. Repeat the same procedure with the other bottle in front of an audience to get them to say, "Wow!" Since the column is just normal ice, feel free to sample it.

The Science Behind It

There are two things going on here. First, the salt is added to lower the temperature of the ice. Adding salt causes the *freezing point* to go lower, so the bottles of water cool below the normal freezing temperature of water, 32°F (0°C). This is the same reason we add salt (or salt water) to roads and sidewalks in the winter to keep ice from building up.

So now you have a bottle of water that is colder than the freezing point, but not frozen. This is called a *super-cooled fluid*. The water doesn't freeze because purified/distilled water doesn't have any impurities. Tap water would freeze. Ice crystals form around **nucleation points**. A nucleation point can be an impurity in the water or a physical impurity, like another ice crystal.

When the super-cooled water hits the ice cube on the plate, ice crystals begin to form. New ice crystals form on the older ice crystals, and your water stalagmite grows. You can even shake the bottle to get the water inside to freeze in a matter of seconds. Now you know the secret to Quick Freeze Ice.

Swing Your Partner

Make a swing move without touching it.

From the Junk Drawer:

- ☐ String
- ☐ Ruler
- ☐ Scissors
- ☐ 2 same-sized washers or fishing weights
- ☐ Tape
- ☐ 2 chairs

Step 1: Use your ruler to measure and cut three pieces of string, each 24 inches long. Tie the end of one string to a washer or fishing weight. Tie the end of another piece of string to the second washer. (Any two objects will work, as long as they are the same size—toy cars and batteries will also work in place of the washers, but they will need to be attached to the string with tape.) These are your pendulum strings. Measure 8 inches in from the end of your third 24-inch-string, and tie the loose end of one pendulum string there. Attach your other pendulum string 8 inches from the opposite side of the third string. Keep the lengths of the two pendulum strings as equal as possible. You've created the Swing Your Partner! Now attach the ends of the Swing Your Partner to the backs of two chairs with tape, or tape them to the edge of a table. Just make sure the ends are at equal height.

Step 2: Now pull one of the pendulums **perpendicular** to the top string and let it swing downward. Watch what happens.

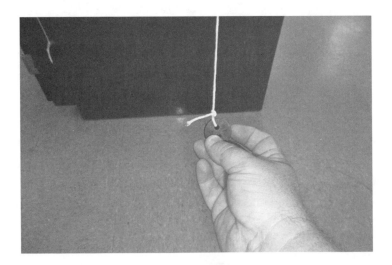

The Science Behind It

Resonance is defined as the building up of large vibrations by the repeated application of small vibrations. The most common instance of this is when you "pump" your legs on a swing set. Adding the small pumping vibration causes your overall vibration (swing height) to get bigger. Each swing of one pendulum of the Swing Your Partner device causes the other pendulum to get a larger vibration. The two pendulums transfer this resonant energy back and forth between them.

Wobble Ball

Roll the wackiest ball down a ramp.

From the Junk Drawer:

- ☐ Hollow plastic ball that you can open
- ☐ Large marble or steel ball
- ☐ Honey
- ☐ Ramp
- ☐ Small ball or marble

Step 1: Find a hollow plastic ball that opens. Small toys often come in these, and the ball is meant to be thrown out; here's a better use for it. The pictures that follow use a Heroics ball, which came with a miniature superhero inside. Squinkie balls will work, but they are small. Star Wars Pods balls will also work. Craft stores sell larger diameter balls (2 to 3 inches) that you can fill for craft projects.

Open the plastic ball and put the heavy marble or steel ball inside it. For the one pictured, I used a large "shooter" marble. Steel balls, like those from a pinball machine, also work well.

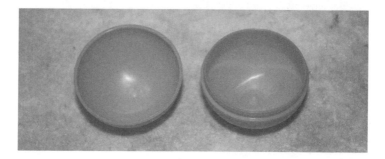

Step 2: Pour honey into the ball until the bottom half is almost full. Close the two halves of the outer ball. This is your Wobble Ball.

Step 3: Make a ramp to roll the ball down. A piece of cardboard or a cookie sheet lifted with some books under one end makes a great ramp. The ball may accidentally open up and create a honey mess, so choose a surface that will clean up easily (like tile). Place the Wobble Ball at the top of the ramp and let it roll down. Observe the motion. Also roll a normal ball or marble down the ramp to compare. Roll your creation across the floor and watch it wobble. This ball is so neat, you should use it to amaze your friends and your parents.

The Science Behind It

Honey is a very **viscous** material. In simple terms, that means it is really thick. The thick honey keeps the interior ball at one side of the plastic ball for a few seconds. That prevents the ball from rolling like a normal ball does. The honey keeps the inside ball off center. Since the inside ball is off center, the ball will wobble as it rolls.

You can also try different types of thick liquids in the ball. Try ketchup, pancake syrup, and dish soap. Different liquids will give different wobbles. Clean up when you are done.

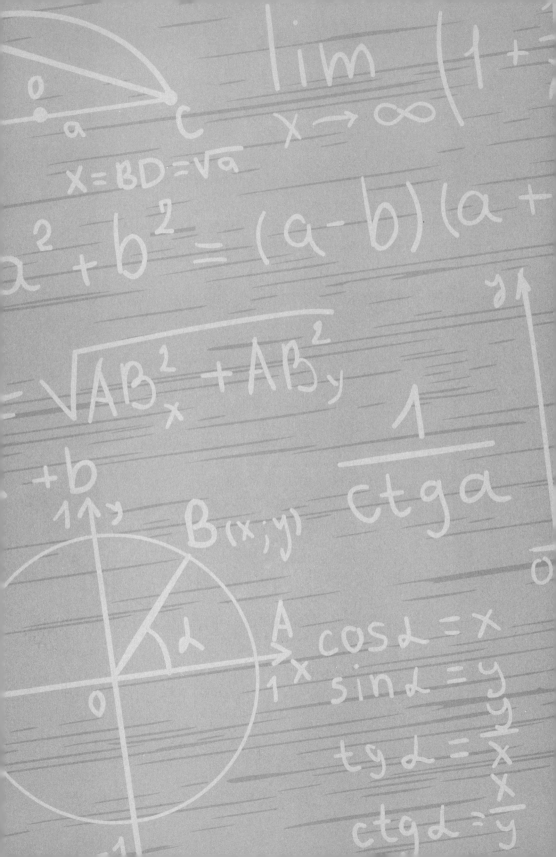

$$\lim_{x \to \infty} \left(1 + \right.$$

$$x = BD = \sqrt{a}$$

$$a^2 + b^2 = (a-b)(a+$$

$$= \sqrt{AB_x^2 + AB_y^2}$$

$$+ b$$

$$\frac{1}{ctg\alpha}$$

$$B(x;y)$$

$$\cos\alpha = x$$

$$\sin\alpha = y$$

$$tg\alpha = \frac{y}{x}$$

$$ctg\alpha = \frac{x}{y}$$

3

Sound and Waves

Straw Oboe

Create a crazy musical instrument out of a drinking straw.

From the Junk Drawer:

☐ Drinking straw   ☐ Scissors

Step 1: Cut a *V* at the end of a drinking straw using a pair of scissors, as shown. This *V* will be the "reed" of your Straw Oboe.

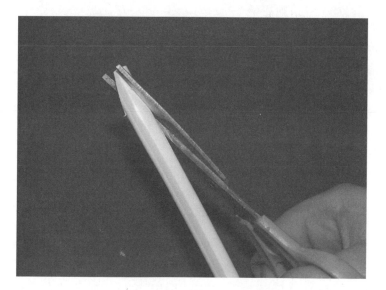

Step 2: Use your teeth to flatten out the *V* end of the oboe.

Step 3: Now place the point of the oboe inside of your lips. Close your lips (but not your teeth) around the *V* of the Straw Oboe. Blow. Vary the pressure of your lips until you hear the sound. You may need to use your teeth to flatten the *V* some more. Trial and error will get you to the correct sound (a loud buzz). Once you have mastered making the sound, you can make Straw Oboes of different lengths (which will create different sounds) or you can try your hand at the next instrument, the Straw Trombone (page 58).

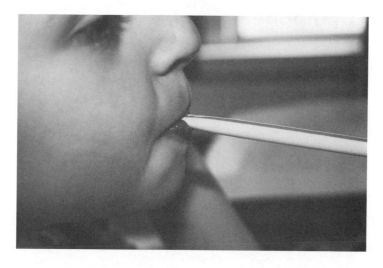

The Science Behind It

All sound is created by *vibrations*. The reed vibrates because of the air passing through it. This creates a standing wave of air inside the straw. Shorter straws create higher frequency sounds. The piccolo is a very short instrument and creates high frequency notes. The tuba is long and creates low frequency notes.

All sound is caused by vibrations. The human ear can detect frequencies from about 20 to 20,000 vibrations per second. Dogs' eardrums can vibrate faster, so they hear sounds at frequencies above what we hear. Ringing bells and sirens are annoying to dogs because of the high frequency sounds we cannot hear.

Straw Trombone

Use two drinking straws to make an even crazier musical instrument than the Straw Oboe.

From the Junk Drawer:

□ 2 drinking straws with slightly   □ Scissors
   different diameters

Step 1: Master the Straw Oboe (page 55) before trying this instrument. You need two straws of slightly different diameters, but the closer in diameter, the better. Cut a *V* in the straw with the larger diameter and get it to play music, like the Straw Oboe.

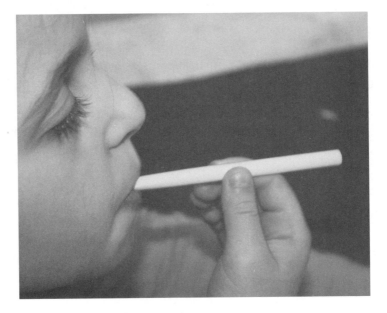

Step 2: Slide the thinner straw inside the uncut end of the larger one. Play your Straw Trombone by holding the large straw with one hand and the thinner straw with the other. Slide the thinner straw in and out as you blow. Practice, and you can even learn how to play songs.

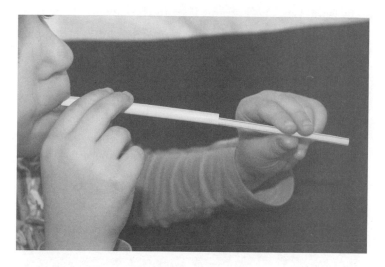

The Science Behind It

As with the Straw Oboe, the vibrating reed causes the air inside the straw to vibrate. By sliding the straw you are creating different lengths. And different lengths give you different musical notes. The frequency of a sound is directly related to the musical note.

Wave Machine

Tape and drinking straws can be used to create a fun wave machine.

From the Junk Drawer:

☐ Roll of masking tape   ☐ Straws
☐ Ruler   ☐ Scissors

Step 1: Tear off a three-foot-long piece of masking tape. Lay the tape on a table, sticky side up; bend one end under and attach it to the table, if the table has a smooth top that won't be hurt by the tape residue. (Don't do it on a fancy wood table.) You could also attach one end of the tape to the underside of a table so the sticky side is up. Attach the other end to the table or a chair. The sticky side needs to be up. Place a straw perpendicular to and across the tape and press it down. Put other straws about every 2 inches. Continue adding straws, but leave about 3 inches at each end without a straw, as shown.

Step 2: Tear off another three-foot piece of tape. Place it sticky side down on top of the bottom piece of tape and straws. Use your fingers to press the tape down between each straw.

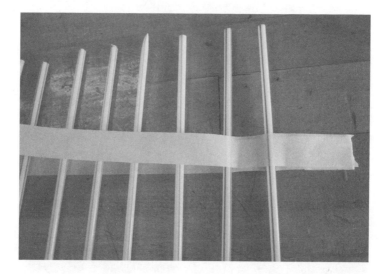

Step 3: Now you are ready to play with the Wave Machine. Remove it from the chair or table and fold the end of the tape over so that no sticky part is uncovered. Repeat with the other end. Tape one end to something solid, like a door knob or the top of a desk. You can also have a friend hold it, but for it to work properly, the Wave Machine needs to be pulled tight. Hold the other end with one hand. Pop down the straw on one end with a fast karate-chop like movement. The wave will move fast. Observe the movement of the ends of the straws as the wave goes down the machine. The ends move up and down only while the energy moves toward the other end.

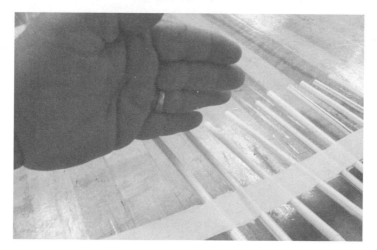

The Science Behind It

Waves come in two major types: **transverse** and **longitudinal (compressional)**. When you chop down, you are creating a transverse wave. The particles of the wave (straws) move up and down, but the energy goes through the Wave Machine to the other end. Waves are just a way to move energy, but the particles in the wave only vibrate. Most waves you encounter are transverse waves. All forms of light and water waves are transverse.

There is one major exception: sound waves. Sound waves are longitudinal or compressional waves. You can create a compressional wave with your wave machine, but it is harder to see. Pull one end of the straw to you, but this time parallel to the direction of the tape. Again the wave will move fast, but watch the ends of the straws. Observe what happens now. In this case the end of the wave is vibrating right to left while the energy also goes right to left. Remember, the particles of the wave just vibrate, but the energy keeps on moving. In both cases, the wave will reflect off the other end and come back to you.

Swinging Wave Machine

Turn a yardstick into a really cool wave machine.

From the Junk Drawer:

- ☐ String
- ☐ Scissors
- ☐ 12 washers (or hex nuts)
- ☐ 2 yardsticks (or pieces of wood at least 24 inches long)
- ☐ Ruler
- ☐ Tape
- ☐ Fluorescent paint (optional)
- ☐ Black light (optional)

Step 1: You are going to create a number of pendulums for the Swinging Wave Machine. A pendulum is a weight swinging on the end of a piece of string or rod. You are a pendulum when you are swinging on a swing set.

Cut pieces of string of the following lengths: 6, 7, 8, 9, 10, 11, 12, 13, 14, 15, 16, and 17 inches long. Tie a washer to the end of each piece of string. You can make more pendulums if you want (or even a few less). If you want to make the Swinging Wave Machine look the coolest, use at least ten.

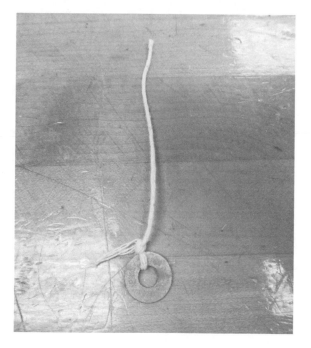

Step 2: Lay a yardstick on a large, flat surface. Put the shortest pendulum at the 1-inch mark. Use a ruler to hang the bottom of the washer so that it is 4 inches below the bottom edge of the yardstick.

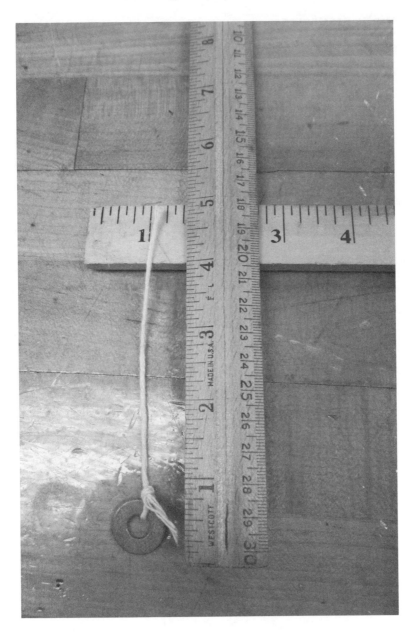

Step 3: Put the next shortest pendulum at the 2-inch mark. Use a ruler to hang the bottom of the washer so that it is 4½ inches below the bottom edge of the yardstick.

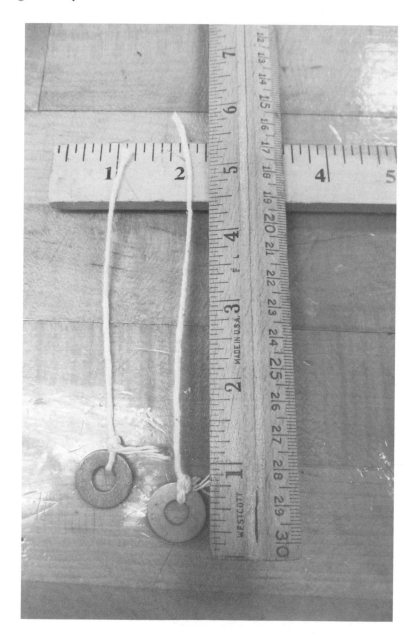

Step 4: Repeat the pattern for the rest of the pendulums. The tops should be 1 inch apart, and each pendulum should hang ½ inch lower than the previous pendulum.

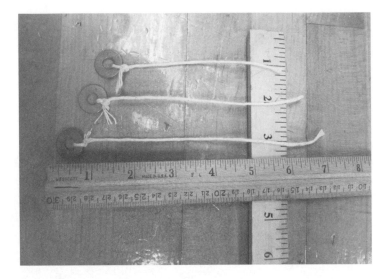

Step 5: Prior to securing the pendulums with tape, your Swinging Wave Machine should look like this:

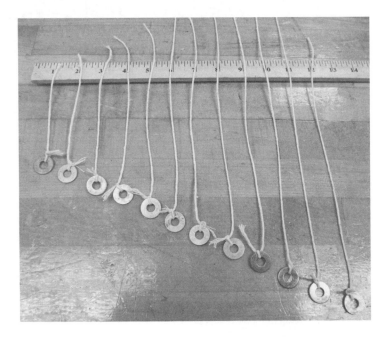

Step 6: Use tape to secure the pendulums to the side of the yardstick. You can do this with one long piece, but several short pieces may be easier to manipulate.

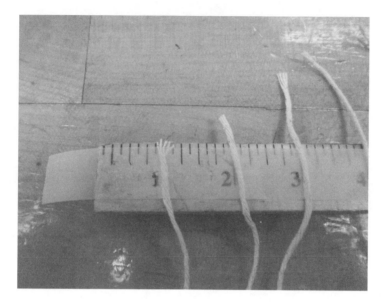

Step 7: Use a second piece of tape to secure the pendulums to the top of the yardstick.

Step 8: Now tape the yardstick to the edge of a table. The pendulums need to be able to swing freely. You can also tape the Swinging Wave Machine between two chairs.

Step 9: Use a second yardstick or piece of wood to push all the washers slowly away from you and hold them there for a second. Quickly pull the ruler toward you, releasing all the washers at the same time, so that the Swinging Wave Machine's pendulums can swing. Enjoy the show. (You can experiment with pushing the second yardstick to different heights.)

Step 10: After you have mastered getting the Swinging Wave Machine to swing, watch it from the end after you get it going. The end view is even more impressive to most people.

Optional Step 11: After you have built it, paint all the washers with fluorescent paint. Fluorescent paint is found in the craft aisle at most stores. Let them dry completely. Use a black lightbulb and use the Swinging Wave Machine in a dark room (except for the black light, of course). This adds a really cool effect to the motion.

The Science Behind It

The time it takes a pendulum to swing is related to the length of the pendulum. Since all the pendulums have different lengths, they will swing at different rates. The short ones swing faster than the long ones. The ripple effect is created because of the gradual increase in length. You are creating one of the most incredible waves you will ever see. Adding the black light allows you to see only the washers and adds to the experience.

Rubber Maraca

A nut in a balloon is all you need to create a noisemaker.

From the Junk Drawer:

☐ Balloon   ☐ Hexagonal nut

Step 1: Stretch out an empty balloon several times by tugging it with your fingers. Insert the hex nut into the balloon.

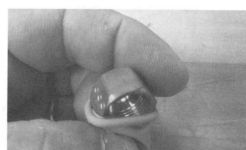

Step 2: Blow up the balloon with the nut inside. Tie the balloon off.

Step 3: The trick is now in the spinning of the balloon. Grasp the balloon in your hand over the neck as shown. Holding the balloon down, rotate your wrist in tiny circles and watch the nut climb the walls of the balloon; listen to the nut's crazy beat.

The Science Behind It

Spinning the balloon exerts a force on the nut causing it to move. The nut wants to go in a straight line but can't because of the balloon. The nut will eventually climb the wall of the balloon and spin around the equator of the balloon. As the nut rolls, each "corner" of the nut rolls into the side and creates a tiny vibration. And vibrations cause sound.

Your ear never stops working. It hears sounds even when you are asleep, but your brain blocks them out.

Rubber Band Man

Learn the secret to guitar strings with just a rubber band.

From the Junk Drawer:

☐ Brand-new rubber band   ☐ Sunglasses or safety goggles
☐ Scissors

Step 1: Cut a rubber band so you have one long rubber piece.

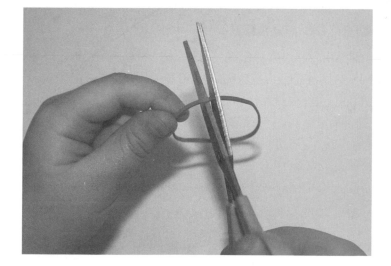

Step 2: Put on your sunglasses or safety goggles. This will prevent the rubber band from snapping back into your eye. It will also make you look like a rock star. Place one end of the rubber band between your teeth. Pull the other end tight—but not so far that it breaks—and pluck it. Pull it tighter as you pluck it and hear how the sound changes.

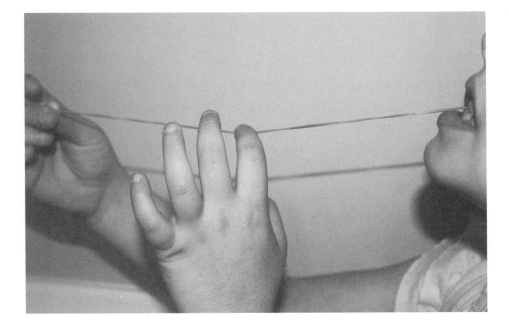

The Science Behind It

There are two things to "hear" from this experiment. First, sound travels better through the inside of your head than through air to your ears. The vibrations transmitted through your jawbone are clearer and louder than anything you hear with air reaching your ears. This is why a recording of your voice sounds different than you normally sound to yourself. You have always felt and heard the vibrations in your head from your talking in addition to the air pressure reaching your ear. The way you sound on a high quality recording is the way you sound to other people.

Second, different *frequencies* are created by different tensions in the rubber band. *Tension* is a pulling force in ropes, cables, and rubber bands. The tighter the tension is, the higher the frequency is. That is how all stringed musical instruments are tuned. The strings are tightened or loosened until the desired musical note is heard.

Sound cannot travel through space. Sound waves must have a substance (like air or water) to vibrate to carry the energy. Astronauts' radios convert the sound into radio waves, which can travel through space, so they can talk to us and to each other.

Air Horn

Wake your neighbors with this incredibly loud mini air horn.

Adult supervision required

From the Junk Drawer:

☐ Empty medicine bottle or film canister
☐ Sharp scissors (or drill and bits)
☐ Balloon
☐ Tape
☐ Drinking straw

Step 1: Thoroughly rinse out an empty medicine bottle (or small film canister). Use the point of a pair of sharp scissors to drill a hole in the bottom of the canister that is the exact diameter of a drinking straw. Or get an adult helper to drill a hole in the bottom of the canister that is the exact diameter of your straw.

Step 2: With extreme care, use the point of a sharp pair of scissors to "drill" another hole into the side of the bottle, as shown. Or an adult can drill the same size hole, though drilling into the side of a round plastic bottle can be dangerous—the bit can slip. You may want to create a small dimple with a knife point or scissor point so the drill bit has a place to start.

DO NOT hold the round bottle while you try to drill into it. Also make sure you are drilling on a piece of scrap wood in case the bit slides off the bottle.

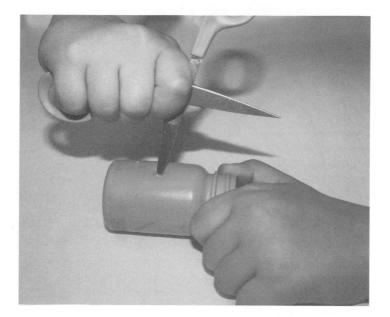

Step 3: Cut a small balloon in half. Stretch the balloon half over the open end of the medicine bottle. You want the balloon very tight and flat.

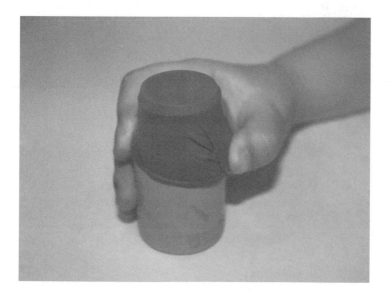

Step 4: Use tape to secure the balloon to the open end of the bottle. Make sure the dimple from the end of the balloon is stretched over the side and taped down.

Step 5: Slide a drinking straw into the hole in the bottom of the medicine bottle. The straw should push slightly into the rubber diaphragm at the other end.

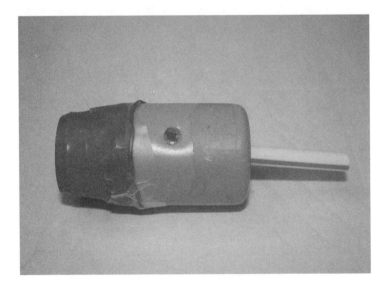

Step 6: You are ready to blow the air horn. The sound will be loud, so be ready. Blow in the hole on the side of your Air Horn. If it is not making noise, try sliding the straw in and out as you blow. Once you have mastered the Air Horn, try different length and diameter straws.

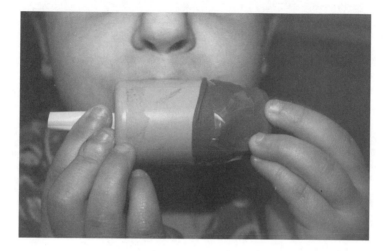

The Science Behind It

Sound is created by **vibrations**. The air rushing in the side causes the rubber diaphragm to vibrate. The vibration creates an air wave in the bottle and the straw. The bottle acts like a *resonator* and amplifies the sound. When the rubber balloon is tight, the sound is very loud. You have created an air horn as loud as a truck air horn powered only by your blowing.

Truck, train, and handheld can air horns work very similarly. Compressed air causes a diaphragm (like our balloon) to vibrate. This vibration creates the sound you hear. It is amplified by going through the horn. Manufactured air horns are louder than the one you made because they use a higher air pressure than what you can create with your lungs.

The crack of a whip is actually the tip breaking the sound barrier. The tip creates a mini sonic boom.

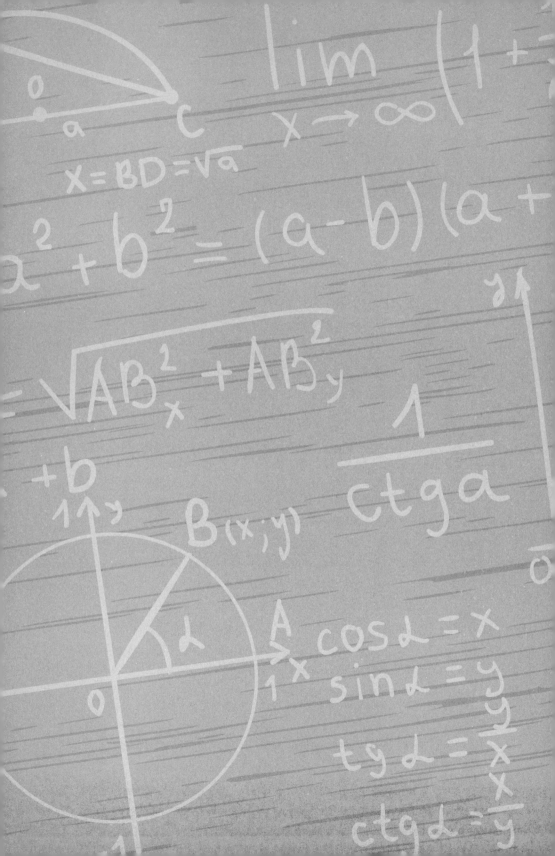

$$\lim_{x \to \infty} \left(1 + \right.$$

$$x = BD = \sqrt{a}$$

$$a^2 + b^2 = (a - b)(a +$$

$$= \sqrt{AB_x^2 + AB_y^2}$$

$$+ b$$

$$B(x;y) \qquad \frac{1}{ctg\,a}$$

$$\cos\alpha = x$$

$$\sin\alpha = y$$

$$tg\,\alpha = \frac{y}{x}$$

$$ctg\,\alpha = \frac{x}{y}$$

4

Light

Pinhole Camera

Learn one of the secrets of light with this fun little "camera."

Adult supervision required

From the Junk Drawer:

☐ Wax paper
☐ Scissors
☐ Disposable plastic or paper cup

☐ Rubber band
☐ Thumbtack
☐ Candle or lamp

Step 1: Cut a piece of wax paper that easily covers the large end of the plastic cup. Pull it tightly over the large end of the cup and secure it with the rubber band. Try to avoid wrinkling the wax paper that is on the large end of the plastic cup.

Step 2: Use a thumbtack or pin to poke a tiny hole in the center of the bottom of the plastic cup.

Step 3: Light a candle (with adult permission). You can also take the shade off a lamp and use the lightbulb as your light source. Turn off the lights in the room. The darker the room is, the better your image will be. Aim the small end of your Pinhole Camera at the candle flame (or lightbulb). Stay far enough away that the cup won't melt. Look at the wax paper end of your Pinhole Camera. You should see an image of the flame. What do you notice about the image? As you move the cup toward the light, or away, the image will change size.

The Science Behind It

Light travels in straight lines called *rays*. The rays from the top of the candle flame pass through the pinhole and go to the bottom of your wax paper "film." The rays from the bottom go through the pinhole to the top of your image. This is why the image is upside-down.

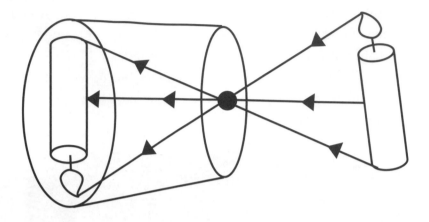

Pinhole Camera Diagram

Scientists call this a *real image* because light actually travels to the point where the image appears. Real images can be projected onto a surface, such as the wax paper. Your eye works the same way. The light goes through the lens of your eye and is focused on the back of your eye just like the image on the wax paper. And it is also upside-down! Your brain flips the image over so you see things right side up. Camera lenses also create upside-down images—we just turn the picture over before we put it in a picture frame.

Up Periscope

See around walls and over couches with this homemade periscope.

From the Junk Drawer:

☐ Cardboard tube   ☐ Scissors
☐ Ruler   ☐ 2 small mirrors
☐ Marker   ☐ Tape

Step 1: Measure the diameter of the end of a cardboard tube. Tubes from kitchen items such as aluminum foil, wax paper, and plastic wrap work best. You can make periscopes with paper towel tubes, but most are very flimsy and won't hold up.

Step 2: Measure down a distance equal to the diameter and make a mark on one side of the tube.

Step 3: Make another mark on the top of the same end of the tube. The mark should be just opposite the mark made in Step 2.

Step 4: Use the marker to draw a line connecting the two marks you made. The line will make a 45-degree angle on the end of the tube.

Step 5: Use scissors to cut along the line you just drew. Take your time, since cutting a thick tube might be difficult. You can always trim it later, after the line is cut.

Step 6: Cut a ¾-inch *V* on the longest side of the cut end of the tube. This will be the eyepiece for the Up Periscope.

Step 7: The Up Periscope shown is created with 1-inch round mirrors that are available in most craft aisles and some dollar stores. Any small mirrors will work, even if they are different shapes, but you might need more tape to secure them.

Check to see if the angle is right. Hold the mirror on the cut end of the tube and look through the *V* eyepiece you cut earlier. You should be able to see the ceiling directly above you. (It might be a good idea to stand under a light fixture or ceiling fan to check this.) Trim the cut end if needed so you can see straight up in the air.

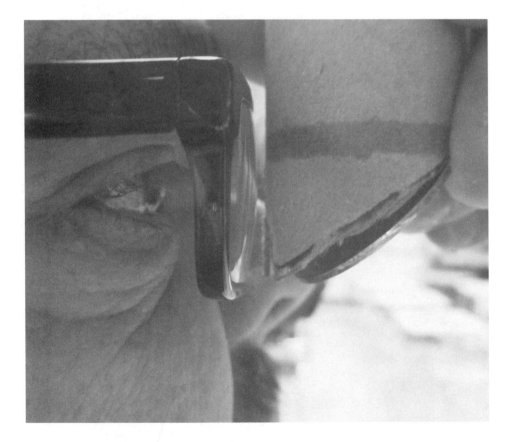

Step 8: Once adjusted, use tape to secure the mirror to the cut end.

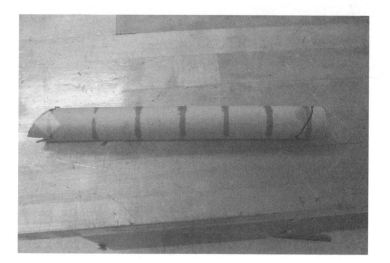

Step 9: Repeat Steps 2 through 5 on the other end of the tube. It is important that the marker line on top is parallel to the mirror you have already taped in place on the bottom.

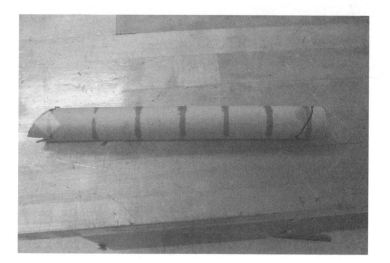

Step 10: Use scissors to cut along the top marker line.

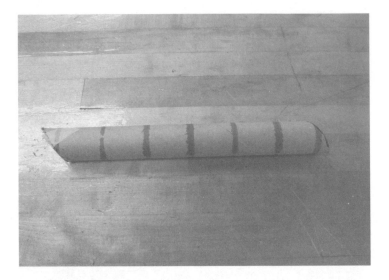

Step 11: You will need to cut a semicircle in the top end, instead of a *V*. It should be on the *opposite* side of the tube from the *V*. You can hold the mirror on the top to test it to see if you want to cut the semicircle larger or not.

Step 12: Once you are satisfied with what you can see, tape the mirror in place. Remember: the mirrors must be parallel.

Step 13: To make the Up Periscope last longer, cover the entire length with tape. You can decorate the tape or buy one of the many crazy patterns of duct tape that are available. Now use your periscope to peer around corners and over couches.

The Science Behind It

Mirrors reflect images we can see. When you brush your teeth in the morning, you are seeing a *reflection* of yourself with the help of the mirror. The top mirror of the Up Periscope reflects the image down the tube, and the bottom mirror reflects the image into your eye.

Periscopes have been used on submarines for years. They allow submarines to stay hidden underwater while the captain peeks above the water using a periscope. Now you can hide and peek around corners with your very own Up Periscope.

Wacky Waterfall

Create a colorful waterfall with a laser pointer.

From the Junk Drawer:

☐ Books
☐ Laser pointer
☐ Tape
☐ Empty 2-liter bottle
☐ Marker
☐ Nail or screw
☐ Water
☐ Bowl or bucket

Step 1: Stack four or five books; the stack should be about 8 inches high. Tape a laser pointer to the top of the books. Use tape to keep the laser pointer on. **NEVER** look directly into the laser, since it can damage your retina. Take the label off an empty plastic 2-liter bottle and place the bottle in front of the laser light as shown.

Step 2: The laser light should shine through the empty 2-liter bottle. With a marker, mark a circle where the laser beam hits the far side of the bottle, the side opposite the laser pointer.

Step 3: Use a nail or screw to create a hole on the mark you just created. A screw works great, since you can move it through the plastic by twisting it. The hole should be about ⅛ inch in diameter.

Step 4: Place your finger over the hole and fill the bottle with water to the top. While keeping your finger over the hole, screw the lid on tightly, and then remove your finger. After a few initial drops, the water should stop coming out! (To learn more about why that happens, try the Super Squirt Bottle on page 164.)

Place the bottle next to the laser pointer with the hole you created on the side opposite from the pointer. Make sure the laser beam is hitting the center of the hole. You may have to add a few sheets of paper towels to adjust the height of the bottle.

Step 5: The water won't drain out until you loosen the top. Put a bowl or a
bucket under the hole in the bottle. Remember, the water is going to come
out in a parabolic (arched) path, so you will have to move the bucket as the
water drains from the hole. Turn off the lights and make the room as dark
as possible. Now loosen the bottle top and let the water run out. You may
have to slightly adjust the bottle so the laser beam stays in the center of the
screw hole you created earlier. The laser beam will follow the bent stream
of water into the catch bucket. It will keep running until the water reaches
the level of the hole.

The Science Behind It

You have just learned the secret of DVD players and most modern surgery. Light travels in straight lines. The laser light is travelling in straight lines but is reflecting off the inside of the water stream. Scientists call this *total internal reflection*. The light follows the curve of the water, even though the beam is actually straight. The straight beam bounces off each side of the water stream and bends as the water bends. If you look carefully near the hole, you may even see the beam bounce off the inside of the water stream in straight lines. Fiber-optic cables use total internal reflection to "capture" a light beam.

Most fiber-optic cables are plastic and look just like clear fishing line. The laser light reflects inside the cable and doesn't escape until it reaches the end of the cable. Pictures and music can be coded onto the laser beam and sent down the fiber-optic cable. Since light moves really fast and experiences almost no loss of signal strength, you can send super clear pictures and music using fiber-optic cables. All DVD and CD players use fiber-optic cables. Bouncing light off the DVD creates the signal sent down the fiber-optic cable. Nothing touches the DVD, and it will last forever if handled carefully.

Fiber optics has also revolutionized surgery. Surgeons now do many surgeries using fiber optics. For example, in arthroscopic knee surgery, they create a tiny incision for a tiny camera and another incision for tiny tools. The doctor sees the inside of your knee on a television set and can move the tools and do the entire surgery through the small incisions. Since the incisions are tiny, you are up and moving much faster. Many surgeries are now performed using this method, and we owe it all to total internal reflection.

Light actually slows down when it goes into a transparent material like glass or water. If the light enters at an angle, the light is bent because of the speed change. This process is called *refraction*. That is why objects are distorted when you look through a water bottle.

Star Gazer

Create a sliding telescope and observe the stars and the great outdoors.

From the Junk Drawer:

- ☐ 2 empty paper towel tubes
- ☐ Scissors
- ☐ Transparent tape
- ☐ 2 magnifying glasses
- ☐ Duct tape

Step 1: Using scissors, split a paper towel tube lengthwise with a single cut.

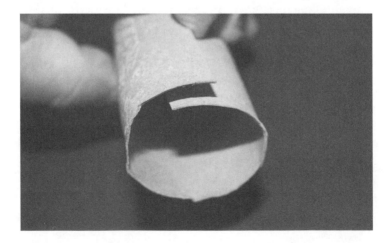

Step 2: Gently squeeze the split paper towel roll so the edges overlap. You want to create a narrower tube that can slide inside another paper towel tube.

Step 3: Use transparent tape to hold the smaller tube together. Tape a strip around the center first. Make sure the tube is symmetrical and add a strip of tape at both ends. Slide the smaller tube inside the big tube to see if it slides easily. If it binds a little (but still moves), that is OK.

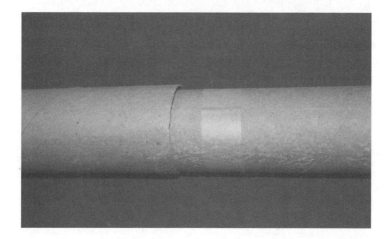

Step 4: Take the tubes apart to do this step and the next one. Use duct tape to attach a small magnifying glass to the end of the smaller tube. If the magnifying glass has a handle, that is fine, and may even make it easier to use. Make sure you don't tape over the entire opening, although a little overlap won't hurt. Note: a great source for cheap magnifying glasses is a dollar store. They usually have three or even four different sizes in one package. They are plastic and will eventually scratch, but they're cheap.

Step 5: Set a larger magnifying glass on a table. (The telescope will also work fine if the magnifying glasses are both the same size.) Use duct tape to tape the larger magnifying glass to the end of the big tube. Small narrow strips of duct tape may make this easier. Tape from the frame of the magnifying glass up toward the end of the tube. After you have secured the glass with four pieces of tape, you can wrap tape around the width of the paper towel tube to better secure it.

Step 6: Slide the smaller tube into the larger tube and you are ready to use your telescope. Hold the large tube with one hand and the small tube with the other. Aim your Star Gazer at a tree or something off in the distance.

Slowly slide the tubes in and out until the object comes into focus. What do you notice about the image? It should be upside-down and larger. Try looking at various things that are different distances away.

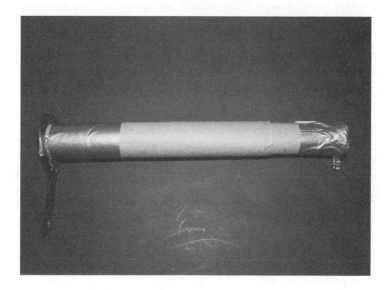

The Science Behind It

Refraction is the bending of light as it passes through a new material. As light from a distant object passes through the first lens, it is bent. When it passes through the second lens, it is bent again. With two lenses (magnifying glasses), you have created a *refracting telescope.*

Light from a distant object passes through the first lens and creates an image. The tree is called the *object* and what you see is called the *image*. Images come in two varieties: real and virtual. A real image is an image that is created by light rays and actually appears on a surface (like the inside back of your eye or a movie screen). When you go to the movie theater, what you see on the screen is a real image. When you look at something with your eye, light passes through your lens and creates an upside-down real image on the back of your eye. Your brain flips the image over. So the first image created by the front lens of your telescope is upside-down.

The lens closest to your eye acts like a good old-fashioned magnifying glass. It magnifies the real image created by the front lens. This second image that you see is called a *virtual image*. Virtual images are what you traditionally see with a magnifying glass. Virtual images are upright and larger, but the only way to see them is to look through the lens. As you look through the eyepiece of your telescope, you see a large virtual image of the upside-down real image from the front lens. The tree appears upside-down. When you use your telescope at night to gaze at the stars, they will be upside-down, and now you know why.

Galileo didn't invent the telescope. He did make a better telescope and used it to popularize science in his day. He discovered craters on the Moon, Jupiter's moons, and sunspots. Many people think his study of sunspots contributed to him going blind in his later years.

What Color Is It?

Learn the secret to colors with flashlights.

From the Junk Drawer:

☐ Clear plastic from a package
☐ Scissors
☐ 3 flashlights

☐ Large red, green, and blue markers
☐ Clear tape

Step 1: Find some clear plastic that is going to be recycled later. Plastic packaging works well. You can use toy packaging, plastic bakery containers, or plastic vegetable containers. Cut three circles that completely cover the front of three flashlights you've found. You can use the flashlights as guides for the circles.

Step 2: Color one circle with a red marker. Large, fat markers work the best. Permanent markers are good, but dry erase markers will also work. You want the color as dark and as even as possible. Repeat with a green and a blue marker for the other two circles.

Note to teachers and homeschool parents: You can also buy cheap colored plastic filter sets. They are great for doing this as a demonstration.

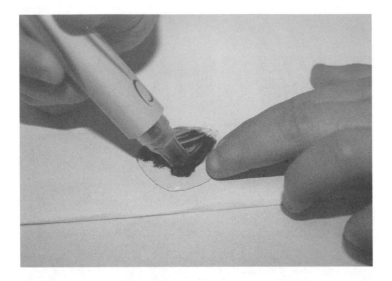

Step 3: Tape one circle to the front of each flashlight. It is OK if the tape goes over the colored plastic as long as it is transparent tape. Make sure no white light escapes. Each flashlight should produce a beam of a single color.

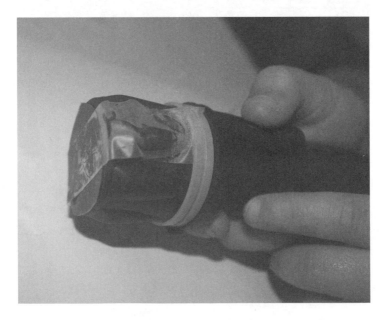

Step 4: Go to the darkest place in your house. A room with no windows works best. A basement or even a closet will work extremely well. If the dark room has plenty of colored objects, you don't need anything but the flashlights. If not, take a variety of colored objects, such as crayons or colored markers.

First, turn on only the red flashlight. Shine it on stuff. What colors do you see? Repeat for the other two colors, one at a time.

The Science Behind It

When light hits any surface, three things can happen: reflection, absorption, and transmission. *Reflection* is when a wave (like light) hits something and bounces off. *Absorption* is when a wave is "captured" into the material. *Transmission* is when a wave goes through a material, like light through clear glass. Transmission only happens with objects that are clear or partially clear (like frosted glass). Reflection and absorption occur with all materials.

White light is made up of colored light. A rainbow is white light being dispersed into colors. The colors your eyes see are based upon what color light is reflected from a surface. Colors are reflected by pigments that are added in the manufacturing process or occur naturally in nature. When white light hits a red shirt, red light is reflected and the other colors are absorbed. That's why the shirt appears red to you. If you shine red light on a red shirt, it will appear red. But when you shine blue light only on a red shirt, it will appear almost black. That is because no red light gets to the red shirt, so no red can be reflected.

Some objects reflect more than one color, like purple, which is a mixture of red and blue. Therefore a purple item reflects red and blue. So in red light only, a purple crayon should appear dark red. In blue light only, a purple crayon would appear dark blue.

An object appears white if all colors are reflected. It appears black if all colors are absorbed.

The collection of all light waves is called the electromagnetic spectrum. Humans only see a small portion, called visible light. Many insects can see ultraviolet (UV) light, which makes flowers appear much brighter to them. Both the insects and the flowers benefit: the insects get food, and the flowers are pollinated, which helps the spread of the flowers.

Crazy Shadows

Create great colored shadows with flashlights.

From the Junk Drawer:

☐ Something to create a shadow

☐ Dark room

☐ 3 colored flashlights (one red, one green, and one blue) from What Color Is It? experiment (page 100)

Step 1: Find an object to create a shadow. An action figure, a coffee cup, or any opaque object will work. Go to a dark room. Basements or large closets work best. You want no extra white light leaking in around curtains and door openings. You can also find a dark bedroom and do this experiment at night. You will need two hands for this experiment, so find a flat surface to put your shadow object on in your dark room.

Hold two colored flashlights, one in each hand. Turn off all the lights except the two colored flashlights. Shine them both at your object. You should see three different color shadows: one for each color and the third one a combination of colors. Repeat for all of the color combinations: red/blue, red/green, and blue/green.

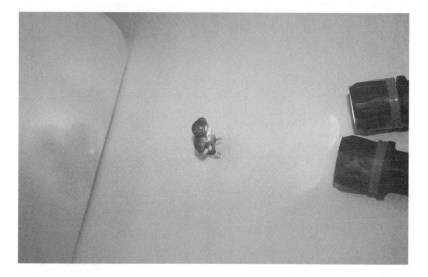

Step 2: Remove the object you used to create the shadow. Now shine all three flashlights at the same time at a wall. You can lay them down on a flat surface if your hands can't hold all three. What do you see where all three lights overlap?

The Science Behind It

When talking about light, red, green, and blue are the primary colors. When different primary colors of light go together, it is called an *additive process*, because the colors of light are adding up. For example, when red and green light shine together, you see yellow. Yellow is called a secondary color of light. Red and blue light create magenta light. Blue and green light create cyan light. Red, green, and blue are the *primary colors of light*. Yellow, cyan, and magenta are *secondary colors of light*. All three lights together create white light. Red, green, and blue light are all that is needed to create every color in your television set. And to create black, just turn all the flashlights off.

For paint colors, *pigments*, the process is a *subtractive process*. The primary pigments are cyan (blue), magenta (red), and yellow. These are the color cartridges in your color computer printer. The secondary colors of light are the *primary pigments*. Cyan pigments absorb red light only. Magenta absorbs green light only. Yellow absorbs blue light only. By changing the amounts of each primary pigment in a material, manufacturers can absorb the colors needed to create the reflected colors they want. We only see reflected light.

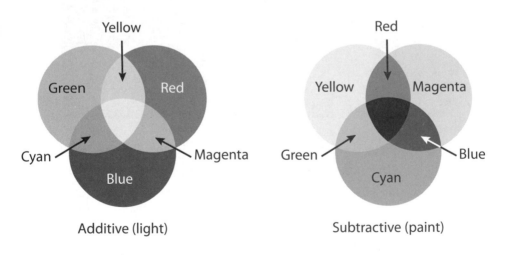

Additive (light)   Subtractive (paint)

Additive and subtractive color combinations

Flash of Color

Use a metal mixing bowl to create blinking colors.

From the Junk Drawer:

☐ Scissors

☐ Large shiny metal mixing bowl

☐ Small bouncy ball (or colored ping-pong ball)

☐ String or thread

☐ Tape

Step 1: Cut a small piece of string or thread to be slightly longer than half the diameter of a large mixing bowl. Tape one end of the string to a small ball. You can actually use any small colored object, such as a small orange, colored ping-pong ball, foosball, etc.

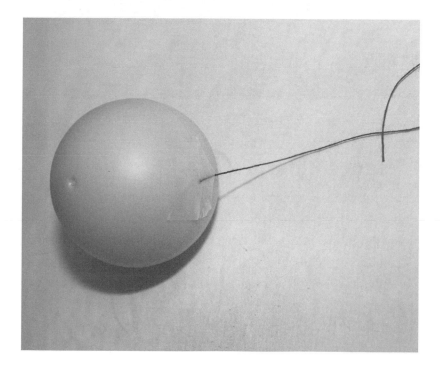

Step 2: Now tape the free end of the ball string to the top of the bowl, so that the ball hangs in the center of the bowl near the back. Move the bowl back and forth with your hand. The ball should swing freely from the thread. The inner surface of the bowl will reflect crazy flashes of color.

The Science Behind It

The metal bowl acts as a **concave mirror**. Concave mirrors are used in car headlights and flashlights. Concave mirrors focus light rays coming in at a point inside the curved mirror called the **focal point**. Headlights and flashlights put an electric lightbulb at the focal point. When the tiny lightbulb emits rays of light, the rays hit the curved mirror and are reflected out in parallel rays, creating a beam of light. In this experiment, when the ball swings, it passes through this focal point and you see a flash of color. Even though the ball is tiny, you will get gigantic flashes of color as the ball passes through the focal point. Try looking into the bowl at different angles as the ball swings and you will see the flashes of color at different points on the interior silver surface.

Capture the Cross

Capture an image with your brain.

From the Junk Drawer:

☐ 2 large index cards (or an old cereal box)

☐ Markers

☐ Tape

☐ Pencil

Step 1: Lay out two large index cards, one on top of the other. You can also cut two equal rectangles out of an old cereal box. Draw a large circle on one using a dark colored marker. A drinking glass (or jar lid) will help you make a round circle. Then use a more colorful marker to draw a small cross on the other index card. Make sure the cross is centered on the card and smaller than the circle.

Step 2: Tape the cards together, back to back. The circle and cross should be facing out.

Step 3: Slide a pencil between the cards as shown, and use several pieces of tape to hold the edges together. To hold the pencil and cards in place, use tape. The easiest way is to angle a piece of tape as shown. Press it firmly in place, then turn the Capture the Cross over and press the tape down to the other side. Tape going over the circle or cross will not affect the activity.

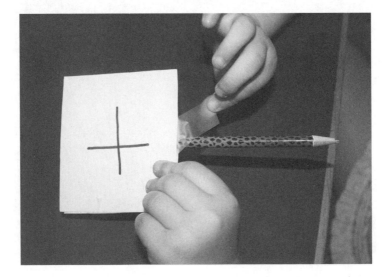

Step 4: Repeat Step 3, but press the tape in the opposite angle. Again, turn over and press the tape down.

Step 5: Place the bottom of the pencil between your palms. Rub your palms back and forth and let the index cards spin. Watch the index cards as they spin. What do you see? You have now captured the cross in the circle.

The Science Behind It

The secret to Capture the Cross is the secret to television, movies, and flip books. When your brain sees an image, it stores it for a fraction of a second. If a new image shows up before the old one is gone, your brain allows you to see a seamless transition. In movies, a new image is shown to your brain before the old image is gone, so you see a seamless movie. You can see how this is done by playing a DVD one frame at a time on your television.

Pringles Planetarium

Create your own star show with an empty potato chip can.

Adult supervision required

From the Junk Drawer:

- ☐ Empty potato chip can with lid
- ☐ Drill and bits
- ☐ Dark construction paper
- ☐ Pen
- ☐ Scissors
- ☐ Wax paper for tracing
- ☐ Small piece of corrugated cardboard
- ☐ Tape
- ☐ Can opener (optional)
- ☐ Pin
- ☐ Flashlight (optional)

Step 1: With adult help, drill a ¼-inch hole in the metal end of an empty potato chip can. You can also use a hammer and a large nail to create the hole. Make sure any sharp edges are pushed inside the can.

Step 2: Lay the can's plastic lid on a piece of dark construction paper. Trace the outline of the lid on the paper and cut out several circles of dark construction paper this size. You want to cut just inside your tracing line so that the paper will fit inside the lid.

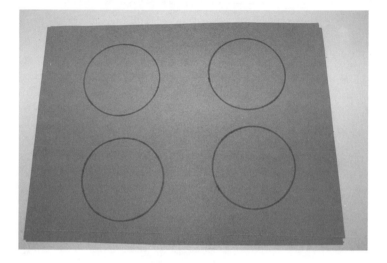

Step 3: Cut out several 3- to 4-inch squares of wax paper for tracing. Lay one on each constellation pattern in the book on pages 116 and 117. Use a pen to mark the location of each star.

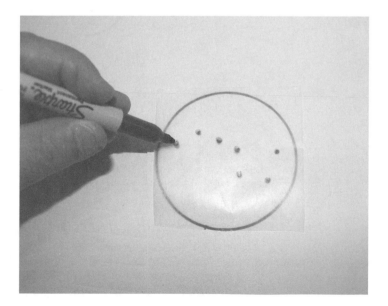

Step 4: Put a piece of scrap corrugated cardboard on the table. On top of it, lay down one of the dark circles from earlier, then lay one of the wax paper constellation tracings on top. You might want to secure the wax paper temporarily with a piece of tape. Use a pin to poke a hole where each star is. Make sure the holes are at least the width of a pencil lead. You can actually use a sharp pencil to make the holes bigger after you remove the wax paper.

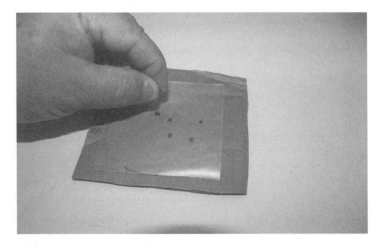

Step 5: Place one of the black constellation circles inside the plastic lid of the chip can. Trim the constellation circle if needed, but it should be very snug.

Step 6: Look through the hole in the metal end of the can and aim at a bright light. Try to name the constellation. To change constellations, simply remove the dark construction paper and replace with a new one. For more constellations, you can go to www.junkdrawerscience.com.

Optional Step 7: With adult help, use a can opener to completely remove the metal bottom of the can. Slide a flashlight into the metal end and center it within the can. A great way to keep it centered is to push tissues or paper towels in around the flashlight. Go to a dark room but try to keep the light switch accessible if possible. Now turn off the light and project your constellation onto the ceiling or wall.

Note to teachers and homeschool parents: You can collect cans and tops with the help of your students. Create sturdier constellation slides by gluing the constellations into the lids. Each group could do one constellation and then trade with other groups. The plastic constellation slides could be kept from year to year and added to. The plastic lids would work with both the eyeball planetarium and the flashlight planetarium.

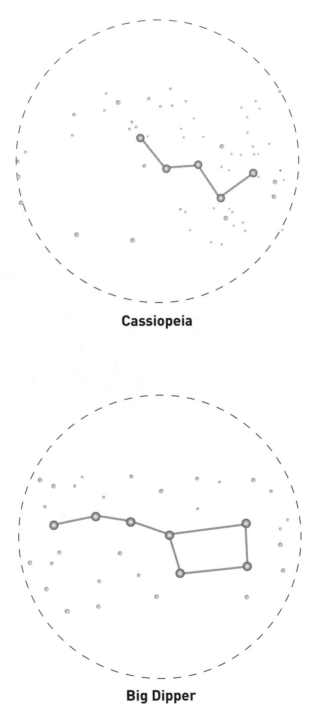

Cassiopeia

Big Dipper

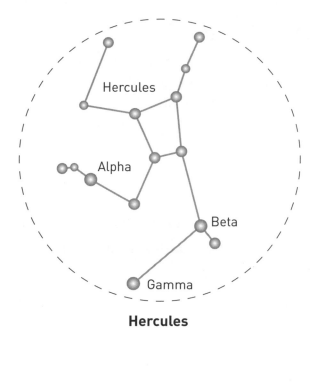

Hercules

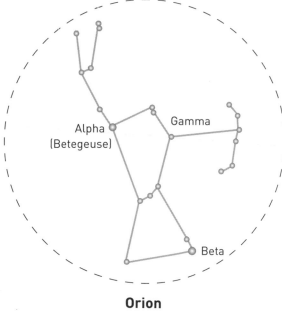

Orion

The Science Behind It

Constellations are groups of stars in the night sky. Before television, books, and video games, people would lie on the ground and make up stories about the stars. Out of these stories came the constellation names. It is a great way to use your imagination, just like looking at clouds on a summer day and searching for shapes. You can even create your own constellation and make up a really cool story to go with it.

> **Light created by the Sun is already over 8 minutes old when it arrives at the Earth.**

Kaleidofoilscope

Make a simple kaleidoscope using aluminum foil and a toilet paper roll.

From the Junk Drawer:

- ☐ Stiff cardstock
- ☐ Scissors
- ☐ Aluminum foil
- ☐ Tape
- ☐ Empty toilet paper roll
- ☐ Scrap clear plastic
- ☐ Pen
- ☐ Sandwich bag
- ☐ Colorful, small objects

Step 1: Cut three pieces of stiff cardstock, each 1½ inches by 3 inches. (Dimensions should work for most standard toilet paper rolls.) You can use index cards, empty cereal boxes, or leftover packaging. You might want to create a triangle like the one shown in Step 6 and dry fit to see if you have the right dimensions for your toilet paper roll. Trim if needed.

Step 2: Cut three pieces of aluminum foil, each about 2 inches by 4 inches. If they are wrinkled, use a smooth glass or rolling pin to make them as smooth as possible.

Step 3: Lay the shiny side of the aluminum foil down on a table. Place the cardstock pieces from Step 1 on top of the foil.

Step 4: Fold the excess foil back around the cardstock and secure with a small strip of tape.

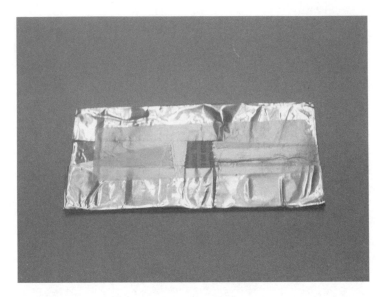

Step 5: Lay all three "mirrors" face down on the table. Leave a very small gap between the three—about the width of a pencil lead. Take a piece of tape and secure the backs of all three together along their long edges.

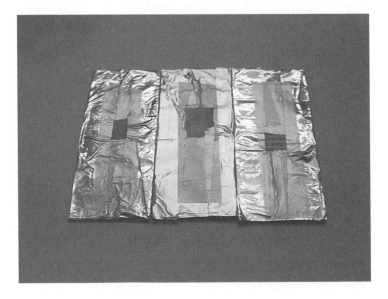

Step 6: Fold the three pieces into a triangle with the shiny sides facing inward.

Step 7: Slide the triangle into the end of your empty toilet paper tube.

Step 8: Stand up your Kaleidofoilscope on a scrap piece of clear plastic. This is a great use for plastic packaging that is almost impossible to open. Trace around the outside of the tube. When you cut out the plastic, you will cut to the inside. This clear plastic piece will sit inside the tube, resting against the foil triangle. You can trim it if it doesn't fit.

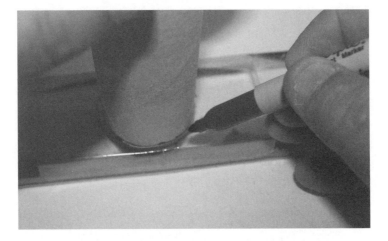

Step 9: Stand up your scope and put the clear plastic piece on top of the triangle of mirrors. Add colorful, three-dimensional things on top of the clear plastic; beads, LEGO pieces, other small toy pieces, and seashells all make great objects.

Step 10: Take a plastic sandwich bag and cut off the ziplock edge. Pull the bag tightly over the end of the tube with your colorful objects. Using both sides of the bag makes it stronger, so use the bag exactly as it came out of the box. Wrap a strip or two of tape around the sides of the stretched bag to hold it in place.

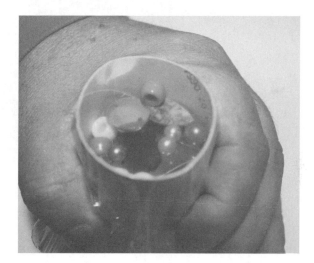

Step 11: Turn the scope over. Take a piece of aluminum foil and fold it over to get double thickness, for strength. Stretch the foil over the eyepiece end and smooth it out. Wrap another strip of tape around the outside to hold the foil in place. Wrap any uncovered portion of the Kaleidofoilscope with tape. Colored duct tape is a wonderful choice, but any tape will work.

Step 12: Use the point of a pencil or scissors to create a hole in the foil for your eye to see through, into the tube.

Step 13: Now pick up your Kaleidofoilscope and look through the eye hole. Rotate the entire scope as you look at a bright light. Enjoy the ever-changing sights you have created.

The Science Behind It

Kaleidoscopes use mirrors to create images. Since you have many mirrors, you create many images. As the kaleidoscope spins, the objects move, and you create a cascade of moving images.

Note to teachers and homeschool parents: The Kaleidofoilscope uses aluminum foil, which does not work as well as a regular mirror. But cutting mirrors is not for kids. You can improve this activity for just a few dollars. Auto parts stores sell actual plastic mirrors that you can cut with scissors—they are used to create custom mirrors for cars. You can also buy mirrored tint, which is shinier; inside the dark scope it works exactly like a mirror. The mirrored tint comes in large rolls that would provide enough for a classroom of kaleidoscopes, as well as the next two activities.

The Never Ending Flame

Make a supercool flame that goes on forever.

Adult supervision required

From the Junk Drawer:

☐ Small picture frame
☐ Clay or Play-Doh

☐ Small mirror
☐ Candle

Step 1: Remove the back and picture from a small picture frame, but leave the glass in. (Secure it with clear tape at the corners if you think it might fall out.) Use the clay or Play-Doh to hold the picture frame upright.

Step 2: Lean the mirror against a rigid support or secure it with clay or Play-Doh. The frame and mirror should be parallel. Stand up the candle directly between the frame and mirror.

Step 3: It helps to turn off the lights as you do this step. The darker your room is, the better the images will appear, but light the candle first (with an adult's permission) if the room will become completely black. Look through the glass frame at the candle. How many flames do you see? Move your head around and watch the flames move.

The Science Behind It

When light encounters a new material, three things can happens. Light can be *reflected* by the material, *transmitted* through the material, and/or *absorbed* by the material. Glass doesn't absorb very much of the light, so most either goes through the glass or is reflected off it. You see the flame due to the light transmitted through the glass. But you also see an image of the flame that reflects off the back mirror. You will see another image that is light from the flame hitting the back of the front glass, reflecting back to the mirror and then finally to your eyes. Depending on the flame size and light in the room, you might see 10 to 12 images of the flame. All that light from only one candle. If you want to see even more images, add some mirrored window tint to the back of the glass . . . or do the next project.

To Infinity and Beyond

Create a cool infinity mirror with a set of holiday lights.

Adult supervision required

From the Junk Drawer:

☐ 8-inch by 10-inch picture frame
☐ Mirror tint
☐ Tape

☐ Similar size mirror
☐ 20- or 25-count string of LED
   holiday lights

Note: Try to use LED lights, since older lights create too much heat. Even with LED lights, leave the lights on only for a few minutes at a time to prevent overheating. If you use old-fashioned holiday lights, they will heat up quickly and could create a fire hazard. **Do this activity under adult supervision.**

Step 1: Cut a piece of mirror tint to fit the glass of your picture frame. You can apply it permanently to the glass according to the tint instructions or just use clear tape to attach it. This creates a two-way mirror that will become the front of your To Infinity and Beyond mirror. Set it aside until Step 3.

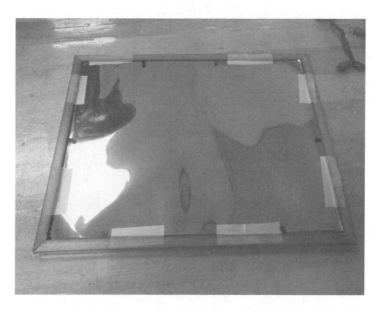

Step 2: Lay the full mirror down on a flat surface, reflective side up. This is going to be the back of the infinity mirror. Starting at one corner, place the lights pointing in and lying flat against the full mirror as shown. Use tape to secure them to the frame. Continue going around the back mirror until all the lights are taped securely.

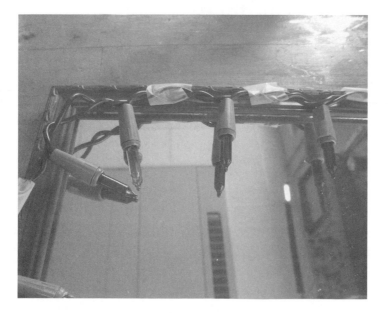

Step 3: Lay the two-way mirror tint on top of the lights and the back mirror. The lights should be sandwiched between the mirror and the tint. Plug in the lights and enjoy the show. Move your head around and watch how the lights "tunnel" into your table. If you have a set of moving or blinking lights, try those for a really cool light show.

The Science Behind It

You have created an infinity mirror. The lights create an image in the mirror, like the candle flame did in the Never Ending Flame activity. This image creates another image and so on. More lights equal more images, and the lights appear to "tunnel" forever.

The mirrored tint creates a two-way mirror. A two-way mirror reflects some light but also lets some light through. A true mirror (like the one in your bathroom) only reflects light. Since the two-way mirror lets some light through, you can see the LED lights. The back mirror (a true mirror) reflects an image of the LED lights back to the two-way mirror. Another image of the lights is created by the light hitting the back of the two-way mirror. This process repeats itself, and you see multiple images of the lights.

Two-way mirrors are commonly used by police departments and store security teams. They work best when one side is extremely dark. A person sitting on the dark side can clearly see through the two-way mirror. On the bright side, light is just reflected, so it looks like a normal mirror. On sunny days, even a regular glass window acts like a two-way mirror. Standing outside your house on the sunny side, you can't see into the house very well—the glass reflects most of the sunlight. But inside the darker house, you can easily see out, since most light goes through the glass. At night, the opposite happens, since it is now darker outside.

Looking in a mirror causes objects to flip from right to left. If you look at the front of an ambulance you will see the word ƎƆИ∀⅃UᗺMA. In the rearview mirror of a car it will read AMBULANCE so you know to get out of the way.

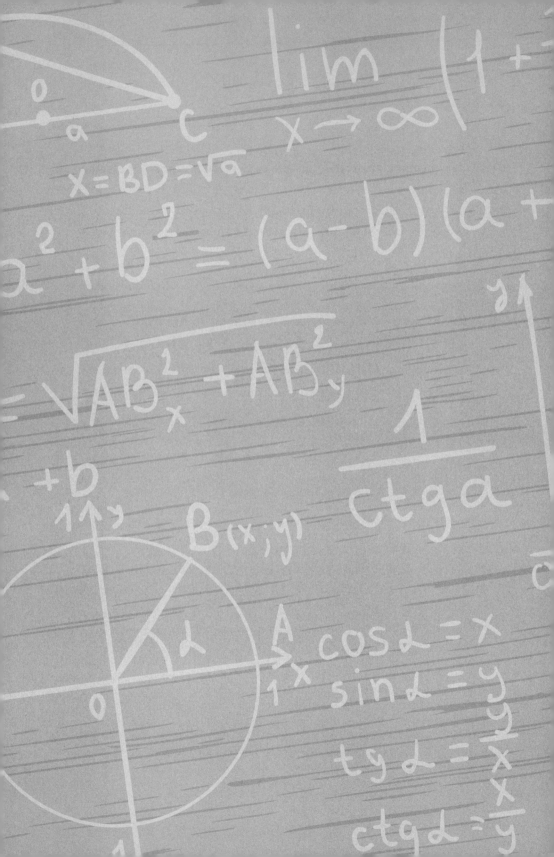

o
a
c

$x = BD = \sqrt{a}$

$\lim\limits_{x \to \infty} \left(1 + \right.$

$a^2 + b^2 = (a - b)(a +$

$= \sqrt{AB_x^2 + AB_y^2}$

$+b$

$B(x;y)$

$\dfrac{1}{ctg\,a}$

α

A

$\cos\alpha = x$

$\sin\alpha = y$

$tg\,\alpha = \dfrac{y}{x}$

$ctg\,\alpha = \dfrac{x}{y}$

5

Electricity and Magnetism

Roll with It Can

Push a can without even touching it.

From the Junk Drawer:

☐ Empty aluminum can
☐ Balloon
☐ Sock or your hair

Step 1: Lay an empty aluminum can on its side on a flat, smooth surface. Blow up a balloon and tie a knot in it. Many people struggle to tie a knot in a balloon, so here is a surefire way to do it: when you inflate the balloon, pull the neck around your first two fingers. Wrap the neck around and slide the neck through the small gap between your two fingers. Finally, pull your fingers out as you tug on the balloon. You have just mastered balloon knot-tying.

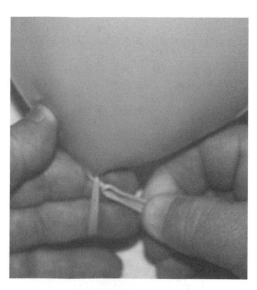

Step 2: Rub the inflated balloon against a fuzzy sock about 20 times. You can rub the balloon with anything fuzzy, like a sweater. Your hair also works well, but when you finish some of you hair will be standing up.

Step 3: Now bring the balloon near the can, but don't touch it, and watch the empty can chase the balloon.

The Science Behind It

All matter is composed of *positive charges* (*protons*), *neutral charges* (*neutrons*), and *negative charges* (*electrons*). Rubbing the balloon causes invisible electrons to be transferred from your sock (or hair) to the balloon. The balloon side you rubbed on your socks is now negative because it gained electrons. The sock is positive, but it is only used to give electrons to the balloon. In electricity, opposites attract and like charges repel. So electrons (negative charges) will attract protons (positive charges) and repel other electrons. Neutrons don't help us any in electricity.

The negative charge will attract a neutral object, like the aluminum can, because the side of the empty can nearest the negative side of the balloon will become positive as negative electrons in the can run away from the balloon. The can is still neutral since the electrons haven't left it, they just moved to the other side. The side of the empty can nearest the balloon is positive and the farthest side is negative. The negative balloon attracts the positive side of the can.

Empty cans on a flat, smooth surface have only a small amount of friction and will roll toward the balloon. As the can rolls, some of the negative electrons continue to shift away from the balloon, so it keeps rolling. The side of the can near the balloon stays positive as long as the balloon is present. When you remove the balloon, the electrons in the can go back to where they started.

Static electricity works best on cold, dry days. If it is rainy or muggy, static electricity experiments don't work as well. High humidity means there is a lot of water vapor in the air. Water molecules are *polar* and have a positive and a negative side. If there is a lot of water vapor, the electrons will jump to the positive side of the water molecules and you won't be able to build up a very good static charge.

There is enough static electrical energy in a lightning bolt to toast 100,000 pieces of toast.

Spinning Straws

Spin a drinking straw in a supersecret style that you can do at any restaurant in America while you wait for breakfast.

I was first shown this experiment a few years ago by a waiter at a restaurant. He did it to amuse my daughters while we waited for breakfast. They were amused, and I added it to my arsenal of static electricity science experiments. He spun the drinking straws on the smooth, rounded top of the coffee carafe that stays on the table during breakfast hours. I tipped him well and would like to extend my thanks to him. I do this experiment in class with the bottom of a very smooth glass.

From the Junk Drawer:

☐ 2 drinking straws
☐ Head of hair

☐ Supersmooth round surface, like the bottom of a glass or top of a coffee carafe

Step 1: Turn an empty glass upside-down. Any supersmooth surface will work. A slightly rounded surface, like the top of the coffee carafe, works even better because it creates less friction.

Step 2: To create a super speed spinner, you just have to use your head. Take both straws and rub them on top of your head about 10 times. Now you are ready to super speed your spinning straws. (You probably don't want to use these straws for drinking after you're done.)

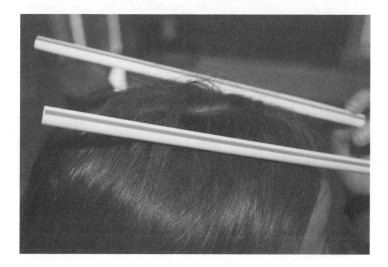

Step 3: Set one charged straw on the upside-down glass. Or set it on the top of a coffee carafe if you are waiting for breakfast.

Step 4: Now bring the other straw close to the balancing straw and watch how fast it spins. Don't touch the rotating straw; just bring the other straw close to it.

The Science Behind It

When you rub the straw on your head, the straw gains a few negative electrons from your hair. Both straws become negative, so they repel each other. The one straw will cause the other straw to spin, since both straws have the same negative charge.

If you watch a friend do this experiment, you will see that the straw is actually attracted to the hair after a few rubs. That is because negative electrons from your hair have gone onto the straw. The straw is negative, since it gained electrons, and the hair is positive, since it lost electrons, so they attract. Like charges repel and unlike charges attract.

Note to teachers and homeschool parents: This may be the easiest way to demonstrate the repelling of like charges. And the students love making their hair stand up with the charged straws.

Super Speed Motor

Use a super magnet and a battery to create an incredibly fast motor.

From the Junk Drawer:

☐ Drywall screw   ☐ Scissors or wire strippers
☐ Small neodymium magnet   ☐ Battery
☐ 4 inches of wire

Step 1: Set a drywall screw upright on the neodymium magnet, as shown. Normal small household magnets may work, but they aren't very strong. If you have a weaker magnet, you will need a shorter screw.

Neodymium magnets are often called rare earth magnets and are found at hobby stores and occasionally the dollar store. They are also the magnet of choice for the magnetic construction toys that you may already have in your house. Many of the rattling magnet pairs sold in the dollar stores also have neodymium magnets in them. You will need adult help to get the magnets out of the toys. If you have an old shake flashlight, it also contains a neodymium magnet.

Step 2: Strip ¼ inch of the plastic insulation from both ends of a 4-inch length of wire. You can use wire strippers or scissors; just be careful to cut through only the insulation and not the wire. It is okay if you cut through the wire, just start over. Wire stripping takes practice. You can find wire in any broken electronic device or at your hobby store. Hang the point of the drywall screw from the bottom of the battery—the magnetic force will transfer through the screw from below, allowing you to do this.

Step 3: Using your index finger, hold one end of the wire to the top of the battery. The battery can be held with the other fingers. With your other hand, lightly touch the other end of the wire to the side of the neodymium magnet. The screw should start to spin. Be careful, since it will spin very fast with a new battery.

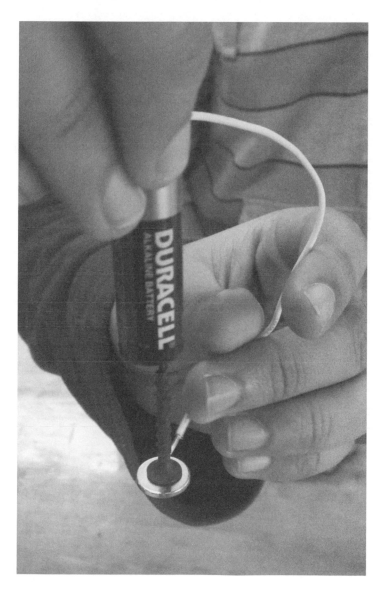

The Science Behind It

When you touch the wire to the side of the magnet, you are completing an electric circuit. Electric current will flow out of the battery, through the wire, through the magnet, and then through the screw back to the negative end of the battery.

The small flat magnet creates a magnetic field, which comes out of the flat sides. The magnetic field is perpendicular to the current flowing through the magnet and it creates a force. The force causes the magnet and screw to spin.

This is called a *homopolar motor* because it always spins in the same direction. This was actually the first motor ever invented, by Michael Faraday in 1821, although his looked a little different. Homopolar motors are quiet and fast, so they are still in use today.

Pencil Lead Lightbulb

Use pencil lead and a few batteries to make your own lightbulb.

Adult supervision required

From the Junk Drawer:

☐ Wire with alligator clips at one end
☐ Scissors or wire strippers
☐ Mechanical pencil lead
☐ Play-Doh, clay, or Silly Putty
☐ Empty glass jar
☐ 8 C or D batteries
☐ Duct tape or electrical tape

Step 1: Find a wire with an alligator clip on at least one end. If you don't have one in your junk drawer, the cheapest place to get one is an auto parts store or the automotive department of a big box store. It is called a "test lead" and can be found by the replacement headlights and taillights for cars.

If you have a lead with alligator clips at both ends, you don't have to strip the wire. You can jump right to Step 3. If you have a wire stripper, use it. But you can easily strip off wire insulation with small, sharp scissors. Hold the scissors in one hand and slightly cut through only the rubber insulation. You want to expose about ½ inch of the bare copper wire. Rotate the wire with the other hand. If you accidentally cut through the wire, that is OK. Just move down the wire and try again. It takes practice to learn how to strip wire insulation.

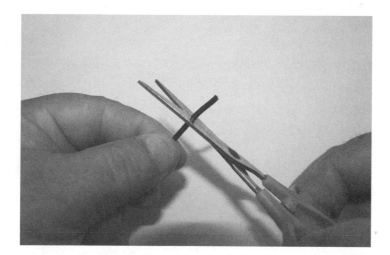

Step 2: With pressure on the cutting edges of the scissors, pull the scissors away from your other hand. If the rubber insulation doesn't pull off, repeat the cut and twist method from Step 1. Again, wire stripping takes practice. Repeat for the other wire. You should have two wires, each with one naked end and one alligator clip.

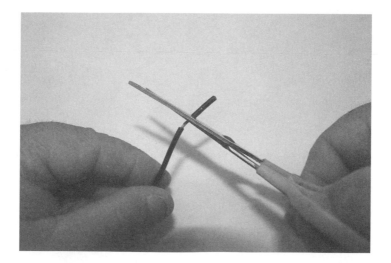

Step 3: Clip a piece of mechanical pencil lead between the jaws of one alligator clip. (Note: Lead from wooden pencils is too thick to work unless you have a power supply that is adjustable.) Use clay, Play-Doh, or Silly Putty to stand this alligator clip up in the air, as shown. Attach the other wire to the other end of the pencil lead. Securing just one alligator clip should be enough to hold both in place.

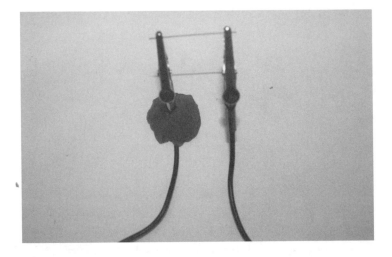

Step 4: Put an empty jar upside-down over the pencil lead "filament" of your lightbulb. The jar allows the filament to last longer, because it restricts the flow of oxygen to the filament.

Step 5: Using duct tape or electrical tape, tape 8 C or D batteries in one long straight line. You are creating a 12-volt super battery. Make sure the batteries are attached positive end to negative end. Use a small piece of tape to secure one wire lead end to the negative end of the battery. If you have double alligator clips on both wires, you will still want to use a small piece of tape to secure the negative end.

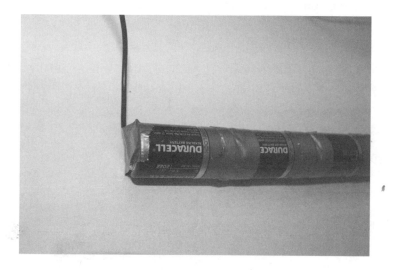

Step 6: Position the other wire so you can easily touch the positive end of your super battery.

Step 7: You need adult supervision for this step. Turn off the overhead lights, since you will light up the room with your own creation. Your finished Pencil Lead Lightbulb should look like this. Touch the wire to the positive end to the battery and hold it there. The electric current will not go through your skin with a battery since it is easier to go through the copper wire. You might need to squeeze the wires to both ends of your super battery to create light in the graphite pencil lead. If you have really thin pencil lead (less than 0.5 mm) and brand new batteries it might even start to smoke. Just let go of the positive end and it will stop smoking. Press harder with your hands and see what happens. If it starts to get really bright it will eventually break the pencil lead and your lightbulb will be "blown."

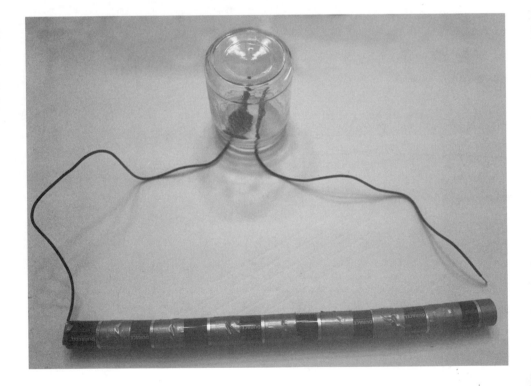

The Science Behind It

All lightbulbs work because electric current passes through the filament. The filament resists the flow of the electrical current and creates heat. The heat creates the light. This type of lightbulb is called an *incandescent lightbulb* and was the standard for over 100 years.

Pencil lead is made of graphite. Graphite conducts electric current and glows. Graphite was used in many lightbulbs before Thomas Edison's time. Thomas Edison made better lightbulbs, but incandescent lightbulbs were around at least 60 years before Edison's invention. His first lightbulb patent was for an improved graphite bulb. As you saw with your Pencil Lead Lightbulb, this type of bulb isn't superbright. Graphite was eventually replaced with different metals, primarily tungsten.

Incandescent lightbulbs are now being replaced with compact fluorescent bulbs and light emitting diodes (LEDs). Both use less electricity to create light, so they are more eco-friendly. They also don't create as much waste heat as incandescent lightbulbs do.

Thomas Edison didn't invent the first incandescent lightbulb; they had been around for over 60 years when his lightbulb hit the market. His company was the first to mass produce lightbulbs, and he did invent the familiar screw-in socket for lightbulbs that we still use today.

Burning Steel

Create your own sparkle and learn about electricity at the same time.

Adult supervision required

From the Junk Drawer:

☐ Steel wool
☐ 9-volt battery

Step 1: This activity will create fire, so it needs to be done on a fireproof surface, such as a cookie tray, outside concrete, or granite countertop. Slightly pull apart the steel wool so it is thin. Press the top of a 9-volt battery into the steel wool and watch the sparks fly. Pull the battery out and the flames will stop.

The Science Behind It

Metal conducts electric current (a moving flow of electrons). The thin strands of steel wool conduct the electrons. As the electrons move, they collide with atoms in the strands of steel wool. These collisions create heat. The heat causes the iron in the steel to heat up and react with oxygen in the air. The reaction actually creates iron oxide, which is better known to us as rust.

All electric current creates some heat, but normal wires are much thicker than strands of steel wool. They don't create enough heat to cause a fire in a normal wire—you never see wires that are that skinny. Most wires would burn if they were that thin. As a matter of fact, because small pieces of iron burn so easy and brightly, tiny bits of iron and steel are one of the most common ingredients in sparklers for the holidays.

The Eiffel Tower in Paris is about 6 inches taller in summer than it is in winter due to the fact that iron expands when it is heated by the sun. Every winter it shrinks back and loses the same six inches.

No-Touch Race Car

Power a car without even touching it.

Adult supervision required

From the Junk Drawer:

□ Toy car
□ 2 magnets
□ Tape (or hot glue, with an adult's permission)

Step 1: Find a toy car that has a flat end. Tape or hot glue a magnet to the flat end of the car. Make sure the car can still roll freely.

Step 2: Find which side of the other magnet repels the car magnet. One side will attract it and one side will repel it. On a smooth surface, use a handheld magnet and the repelling side to push the car around. You can also turn the handheld magnet over to "pull" the car, but it will almost always move too quickly and stick. Flip it back over to the repelling side and drive the car with no hands.

The Science Behind It

All magnets have two poles: north and south. Two north poles will repel each other. Two south poles will repel each other. When you are pushing the car with the magnet, the two sides facing each other are repelling so you can drive the car without touching it. When you flip the magnet and pull the car, the poles are now opposite, so they attract each other.

Crazy Chaos Pendulum

Use magnets to create one of the coolest displays you will ever see.

Adult supervision required

From the Junk Drawer:

- ☐ 7 or 8 magnets
- ☐ Unsharpened pencil
- ☐ Hot glue or superglue
- ☐ String
- ☐ Scissors
- ☐ Tape
- ☐ Cardboard
- ☐ For a permanent option: needle-nose pliers and a metal coat hanger

Step 1: With adult help, superglue or hot glue a magnet to the pencil lead end of an unsharpened pencil. Normal refrigerator-style magnet buttons will work, but the swings are crazier if you have the superstrong neodymium magnets (see page 139).

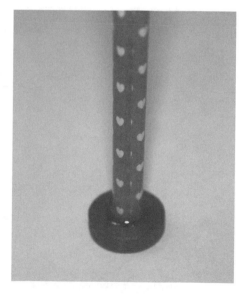

Step 2: Cut a 3-inch long piece of string. Tape approximately ½ inch of the string to one side of the eraser end of the pencil.

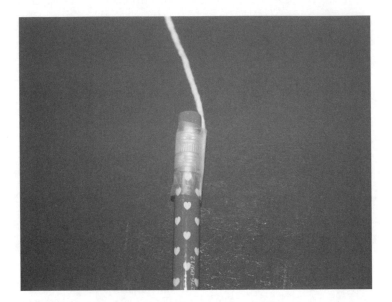

Step 3: Tape the other end of the string to the other side of the pencil so that you have a loop of string. The pencil will be suspended by this loop from your hand.

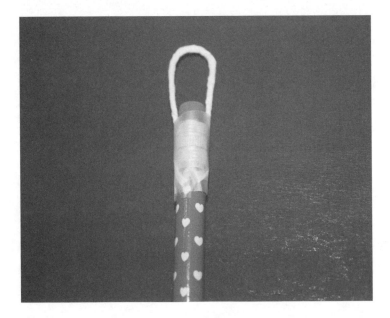

Step 4: Cut a 4-inch square of corrugated cardboard.

Step 5: For the remaining magnets, find out which side repels the pencil end magnet. Bring each magnet close to the pencil end magnet. One side will repel and the other side will attract.

Step 6: Place the magnets randomly on the cardboard square with the side that repels up. Hold the loop of string in one hand. Dangle the pencil about ½ inch above the magnets on the cardboard square. Pull back the

magnet end of the pencil with one hand and let it swing like a pendulum. Experiment by moving the pencil top slightly. You can also try moving the magnets on the cardboard. Flip some of the lower magnets over and see how the movement of the Crazy Chaos Pendulum changes.

Optional Step 7: If you want to make a permanent Crazy Chaos Pendulum, you will need adult help. On the hanger, create a small outward hook with a pair of needle-nose pliers. Grab the middle of the flat bottom of the hanger and pull it to create a diamond shape. Bend the bottom of the diamond to the side so the pendulum hanger will sit flat. Hang the pencil pendulum from the small hook you created. Bend the hanger until it will stand and the pencil magnet is about ½ inch above the magnets on the cardboard. Pull it back and let it swing.

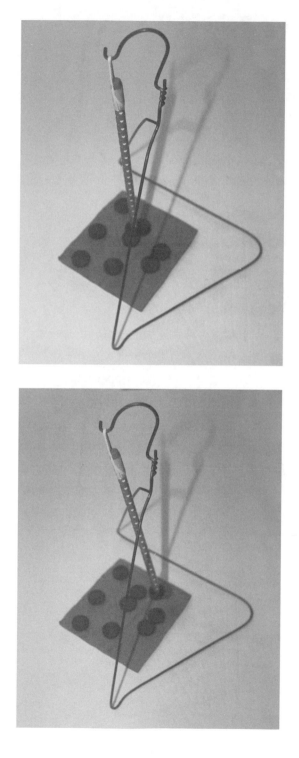

The Science Behind It

All magnets have a north pole and a south pole. Like poles repel each other and unlike poles attract each other. Since the bottom of your swinging magnet repels the top of all the cardboard magnets, chaos results. The Crazy Chaos Pendulum tries to swing like any other pendulum under the influence of gravity, but as it approaches one of the cardboard magnets, it is repelled. The pencil end magnet then swings close to another cardboard magnet and it is repelled again. Try swinging it different directions and moving the cardboard magnets around. Let the chaos begin.

Electric Magnet

Build a simple electromagnet that you can turn on and off.

From the Junk Drawer:

- ☐ Insulated wire
- ☐ Scissors or wire strippers
- ☐ Large nail
- ☐ Tape
- ☐ New battery
- ☐ Paper clips

Step 1: Strip the insulation off the end of a piece of wire. A 10- or 12-inch piece of wire works well. You can use wire strippers if you have them, or you can use scissors. Carefully cut through the insulation only. Slowly rotate the wire until you can pull off just the insulation. Don't worry if you cut the wire on your first try; stripping wire becomes easier with practice.

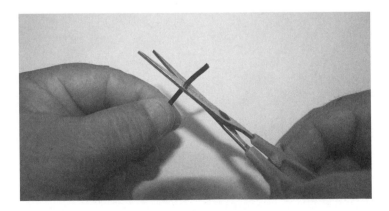

Step 2: Wrap the wire around an iron nail, as shown. Leave the stripped ends hanging lose.

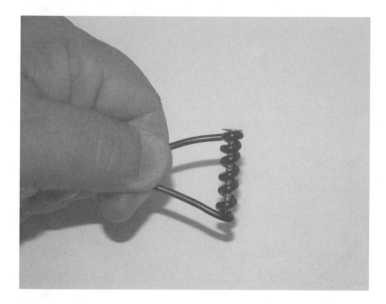

Step 3: Depending on the wire you use, it may uncoil as soon as you let go. If that is a problem, use tape to hold it in place so that your hands are free to do the rest of the activity.

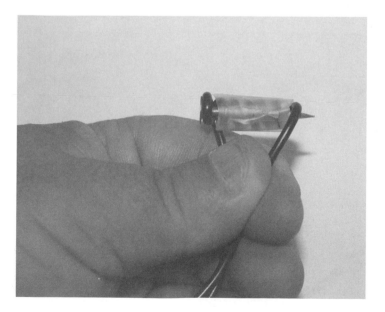

Step 4: Now attach both ends of the loose wire to a new battery. You can hold the wire ends with your thumb and index finger to the ends of the battery. Don't worry, the electric current would rather go through the wire than your fingers, so you won't feel it.

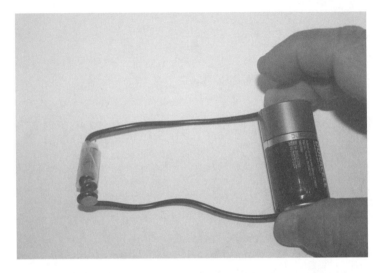

Step 5: Now bring the end of the nail near a pile of paper clips. See how many you can pick up. Let go with your thumb so the wire detaches from the battery and observe what happens.

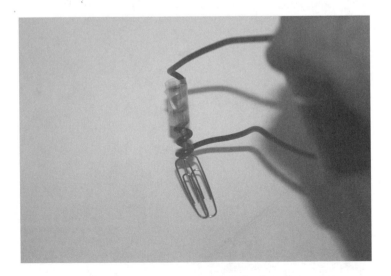

The Science Behind It

In this activity, attaching the wire to both ends of a battery causes electric current to flow through the wire. The current flowing through the wire creates a *magnetic field* in the iron nail. Electricity is used to create magnetism and magnetism is used to create electricity. They are closely related.

Your iron nail becomes a *temporary magnet* because of the electricity. When you remove the battery, the nail is no longer magnetic. Electromagnets are used around us all the time. Doorbells are a common electromagnet in most houses. In most schools, hallway doors are held open with electromagnets. Look behind the open door to see them. When the fire alarm goes off, the electric current to those magnets stops, and the doors automatically close. This would slow down the spread of any fire and smoke. You could still open the door by hand if it was safe.

Thomas Edison was granted over 1,000 patents for his many inventions, including an improved lightbulb. That was a US record until it was surpassed by Don Weder. An Illinois florist, Don Weder has over 1,300 patents, most dealing with better ways to store, sell, or display flowers.

$$O$$

$$c$$

$$a$$

$$x = BD = \sqrt{a}$$

$$\lim_{x \to \infty} \left(1 + \right.$$

$$a^2 + b^2 = (a-b)(a+$$

$$= \sqrt{AB_x^2 + AB_y^2}$$

$$+ b$$

$$B(x;y) \qquad \frac{1}{ctg\alpha}$$

$$\cos\alpha = x$$
$$\sin\alpha = y$$
$$tg\alpha = \frac{y}{x}$$
$$ctg\alpha = \frac{x}{y}$$

$$A$$

6

Fluids and Pressure

Snow Globe

Create your own glitter-filled snow globe from one of your favorite toys.

Adult supervision required

From the Junk Drawer:

- ☐ Empty glass bottle or jar
- ☐ Old toy
- ☐ Glitter
- ☐ Water
- ☐ Hot glue or superglue

Step 1: A wide, fat jar works best. Clean it thoroughly and remove the label. Go through your toys and find a plastic action figure, animal, or any plastic toy that fits inside the glass jar. Test the fit of your chosen toy. If you leave the toy in the water too long, it may fade (or even start dissolving), so choose a toy that is destined for the scrap heap someday.

Pour a container of glitter into the empty jar. If you don't have glitter in your junk drawer, it is available at dollar stores and in the craft section in most stores. Add water to the glass jar. You don't have to fill it all the way, since the toy will take up some of the volume.

Step 2: Get adult help and superglue or hot glue the toy to the center inside of the lid. Let the glue dry completely.

Step 3: Over a sink, invert the lid and screw it down tight. Having a few bubbles of air inside the jar is OK, but you can add more water if you want to remove them. If you get adult to help screw the lid on supertight, it shouldn't leak, but test for leaks over the sink. You can add a bead of hot glue to the inside of the lid and make it a permanent seal if you choose.

Finally, turn the globe over, shake it up, and watch it "snow" on your toy.

The Science Behind It

Objects float or sink because of *buoyancy*. Water applies an upward pressure on all submerged objects that are less dense than water, and downward pressure on objects that are more dense. The tiny pieces of glitter are very close to the **density** of water, but slightly more dense—they will seem to float and swirl in the moving water for a long time, but will eventually sink.

Less dense objects float on more dense objects. It is much easier to float on salt water, such as ocean water, because the density of salt water is greater than the density of fresh water.

Super Squirt Bottle

Squirt your friends with this great toy.

From the Junk Drawer:

☐ Empty plastic drink bottle   ☐ Water
☐ Screw

Step 1: This activity is best done outside, since stuff will get wet.
Rinse out a plastic drink bottle. Use a screw to "drill" a hole in the side. Twist the screw and it will eventually drill through the plastic.

Step 2: Place your finger over the hole and fill the bottle with water. Keeping your finger over the hole, screw the cap on tightly. Remove your finger and only a few drops should come out.

Step 3: While pointing the hole away from you, squeeze the bottle and watch the water squirt out. Aim at your friends and have fun. You have just created the world's cheapest squirt toy.

The Science Behind It

The water won't come out the hole when the top is on tight. Why? The cap is the key. The cap prevents air from pushing on the top of the water. Since air doesn't rush in the top of the bottle, the air pressure on the hole is the same as the water pressure. The water stays inside. If you remove the top, the water will run out.

But when you squeeze the Super Squirt Bottle, you are applying *pressure* to the walls of the bottle. The additional pressure is transmitted through the water. The additional water pressure at the hole wins, and the water squirts out.

Try squeezing harder and watch what happens. At your next summer picnic, create a few as a fun way to learn science and a great way to cool off.

Falling water could take any shape, but it forms a teardrop shape. The teardrop is the most streamlined shape possible.

Plumber Strength

Use a plunger for an amazing feat of strength.

From the Junk Drawer:

☐ Bathroom plunger (clean)
☐ Chair or stool with flat top

Step 1: Press a clean plunger down on the flat top of a chair or bar stool. Press until air squishes out from under the plunger. This activity will not work with upholstered chairs.

Step 2: Lift up on the plunger handle. You may need to use both hands, depending on the chair. Your amazing strength has lifted the chair with an assist from air pressure.

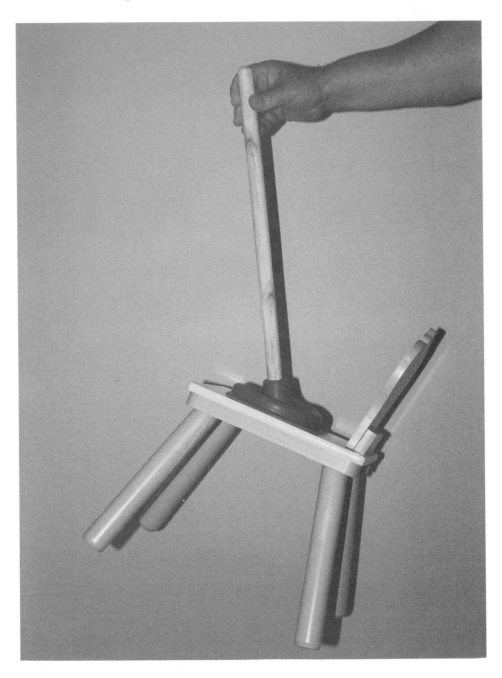

The Science Behind It

Air pressure is amazing. When you press down on the plunger, you press out air. Under the dome of the plunger, you now have less than normal air pressure. Under the chair, you still have normal air pressure. The extra air pressure under the chair helps to lift the chair.

Unspillable Water

Make water go where you want it to, using string.

Junk Drawer Stuff:

☐ String

☐ Water

☐ 2 cups

☐ A safe place to get wet

Step 1: You need to do this activity on an outside patio table or over a sink. Any place that is safe to get wet will work.

Take a piece of string about 2 feet long and submerge it in water. The string needs to be extremely wet.

Step 2: Pull one end of the string out of the water and put it in the empty cup. Lift the cup full of water above the other cup. Pull the cups apart until the string forms an angle from the elevated full cup down to the empty cup on the table, as shown. Using a measuring cup as the top cup makes it easier, since a measuring cup has a pour spout, but it will work with any two cups.

Step 3: Slowly tilt the top cup until the water makes a very thin trickle out of the top cup. Watch as the water follows the string. You can even move the top cup as you pour. The water will follow the string as long as you don't tilt the top cup too much. (You can use an index finger to hold the top string in place if needed.)

The Science Behind It

Water is a *polar molecule*. That means one end of the H_2O molecule is positive and the other is negative. Water molecules look like Mickey Mouse's head. The hydrogen atoms are the ears (there are two of them) and the round face is the oxygen atom. The hydrogen atoms are positive, so the end with the ears is positive. The end with the face is negative. Since opposite charges attract, the water molecules want to stick together in nature. Positive ears stick to the negative face of the next molecule over, so the water holds together. This is the reason for *surface tension* in water. Just don't tip the top cup too much or you will end up all wet, because if you pour out too much water (mass), gravity will take over and the water will fall straight down.

Water can defy gravity. Put a corner of a dry washcloth into a bathtub of water and the water will climb up the washcloth. This process is called *capillary action.*

Tornado in a Bottle

Create a tornado in your house

Adult supervision required

From the Junk Drawer:

- ☐ 2 empty soda bottles and caps
- ☐ Superglue or hot glue
- ☐ Drill and bits
- ☐ Scrap piece of wood
- ☐ Duct tape

Step 1: Clean and rinse out two plastic drink bottles that match. Smaller drink bottles, 16 or 20 ounces, are easier to handle. With an adult's help, use superglue or hot glue to stick the two bottle caps together. The flat side of the caps should face each other. Let them dry completely before going to the next step.

Step 2: Get adult help to use the drill. Use a ½-inch bit to drill a hole in the center of the two bottle caps, but place a scrap piece of wood under the caps as you drill through the center.

Step 3: Wrap a strip of duct tape around the center of the two caps for added support.

Step 4: Fill one bottle completely full of water. Screw the cap onto the full bottle. Turn the empty bottle upside-down and screw it onto the two cap arrangement.

Step 5: For even more support, wrap another piece of duct tape around the glued bottle caps. This should be a full-width strip of duct tape.

Step 6: Invert the Tornado in a Bottle. Swirl the top bottle in a small circle. After you swirl it a few times, you can stop and let the fun begin. The water in the top bottle should start making a tornado as it empties into the bottom bottle. It will take some practice to get good at it. But you can keep inverting it and trying again until you get the swirl just right.

The Science Behind It

As you swirl the bottle, you are creating a whirlpool. Scientists call this a *vortex*. The vortex spinning causes the water to spin. The spinning water creates an area of low pressure air at the center of the vortex. This low pressure area in the top bottle pulls air upward out of the bottom bottle. Air will always flow from high pressure to low pressure. Gravity is also pulling water down into the lower bottle. The water drains out very quickly.

   Note to teachers and homeschool parents: This is a great activity to use when discussing tornadoes, vortexes, and pressure. It is easy to make with smaller bottles so every student can have their own to take home. Have the students drain them before taking them home; they can refill them there. In the classroom, hot glue works the best. Wrapping a strip of duct tape around the area where the two caps are joined is also helpful. Between the glue and the tape, leaks are avoided.

Pop Bottle

Pop a bottle in the name of science.

From the Junk Drawer:

☐ Empty eco-friendly thin water bottles

Step 1: This trick works best with the newer thin water bottles. Empty a bottle by having a drink of water. Screw the lid back on the empty bottle, but only enough to hold the top on—do not make it supertight. You might have to experiment to find the right amount of twist.

Step 2: Begin twisting the bottom of the bottle with one hand as you hold the top of the bottle with your other hand. Aim the bottle away from friends, pets, or anything breakable. Keep twisting until the bottle is really tight. Now use your thumbs to slightly twist the top and watch it pop off.

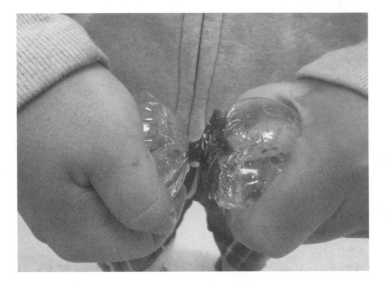

The Science Behind It

The top pops off because of air pressure. You have a trapped amount of air in the bottle. As you twist the bottle you are increasing the air pressure inside the bottle by decreasing the volume the air occupies. Eventually, the force from the air pressure overcomes the friction holding the top on, and it pops off.

This experiment works best with the thin-walled water bottles because they are easier to twist. (This experiment will work with thicker soda bottles, but you have to be really strong to twist them.) The walls are thinner to save plastic, and because there is no dissolved carbon dioxide in the water. Soda bottles need thicker walls because of the carbon dioxide gas in them, which generates greater pressure inside the bottle. Carbon dioxide is the great fizz in soda pop.

Ketchup Diver

Make a midget submarine from leftover condiments.

From the Junk Drawer:

☐ Ketchup packet   ☐ Water
☐ Empty 2-liter plastic bottle

Step 1: Not all ketchup packets will work for this experiment, but most will. Hunt's packets work, but the ones from the golden arches do not. A packet that works will float almost completely submerged when unopened.

Once you find a packet that works, here is what you do. Fill an empty 2-liter bottle about ¾ of the way full with water. Squeeze the packet through the opening and screw the cap on as tightly a possible.

Step 2: Squeeze the bottle hard with your hands. You might need two hands to create enough force. Watch the ketchup packet dive. Let go and watch it rise. Try varying amounts of pressure. With practice, you can get the ketchup to stop in the middle.

The Science Behind It

You have created a fun device called a Cartesian diver. Objects float because of their density. Density is equal to mass divided by volume. Objects with a density lower than that of water float.

The ketchup packet floats because its density is initially less than the density of water. The density is less than that of water because of a small amount of air trapped inside the packet. When you press on the sides of the bottle, you increase the pressure in the water, and this increased pressure is transmitted throughout the liquid. The increased pressure causes the air inside the ketchup packet to become slightly smaller. The smaller packet now has a density greater than the surrounding water, so it sinks. When you get the packet to float in the middle, the density is momentarily equal to the density of water.

Double Trouble

Use two balloons to amaze yourself and challenge your friends.

Adult supervision required

From the Junk Drawer:

☐ 2 pop-up-top bottle caps   ☐ Duct tape
☐ Hot glue (and/or duct tape)   ☐ 2 balloons

Step 1: Find two pop-up-top bottle caps. These are found on some water bottles, sports bottles, and various juice bottles, like Bug Juice and Belly Washers. This is a perfect reason to buy cool character pop-up tops, like Iron Man.

　　　With adult help, place a bead of hot glue around the bottom edge of one of the bottle caps.

Step 2: While the glue is still hot, push the two caps together, being careful not to touch the glue with your fingers.

Step 3: Wrap a strip of duct tape around the caps to seal the joint. If you have really good duct tape, you can actually just tape the two tops together and skip the hot glue completely.

Step 4: Push both pop-up tops in before connecting the balloons. Blow up a balloon **completely** and stretch the neck over one of the pop-up caps. **Slightly** inflate another balloon and place it over the other pop-up cap.

Step 5: Make a prediction about what will happen when you open both pop-up tops. Will the balloons inflate to equal size? Will the big one get bigger and the small one go completely empty? Will the little one get smaller and the big one get bigger?

After making a prediction, pop up both caps so air is free to move between the two balloons. Pretty amazing, and not what you initially thought would happen, right? Don't worry. Almost everybody gets it wrong until they know the science. Read on to learn more.

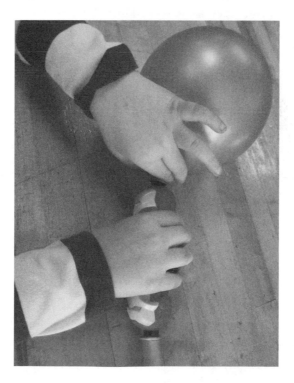

The Science Behind It

Air naturally moves from higher pressure to lower pressure. The pressure in the balloons is created by the rubber of the balloon. The balloon has a finite number of rubber molecules. When most of the air empties, the balloon is very thick—there are many rubber molecules side by side. There are lots of elastic molecules tugging on each other so there is more force from the balloon wall. More force equals more air pressure.

As the balloon inflates, the rubber molecules stretch out as the balloon wall gets thinner, with fewer molecules side by side, which means less force from the rubber. Less force equals less air pressure from the balloon wall. That's why the partially filled balloon empties some air into the bigger balloon.

You can observe this in action every time you blow up a balloon. The thick wall at the beginning makes it hard to start blowing it up—your lungs have to exert a greater pressure. But as the rubber stretches, it becomes easier to inflate the balloon.

Now, go amaze your friends with this neat trick. Almost everybody gets this wrong the first time they see it, so be kind. After all, you already know the science.

Air rushing over an airplane's wing gives the airplane *lift* and allows it to fly. A spoiler on a race car is an upside-down wing. As the car speeds up, the inverted wing creates *down force* (the opposite of lift). Down force allows a race car to go faster in the corners.

Appendix

How do I fill my junk drawer with great science supplies?

Most of the items for *Junk Drawer Physics* are probably already in your house. But a few might be less common. Dollar stores are a great first option. Magnifying glasses and mirrors are great dollar store items. Walking the aisles of a good dollar store will lead to a treasure trove of supplies. Home improvement stores are great for mirrored tint and dozens of other items. Craft stores are loaded with different types of magnets and many other useful items. The grocery store is a great option for straws and pie pans.

Teachers, scoutmasters, and youth counselors may need multiple sets of the *Junk Drawer Physics* items for labs. As a matter of fact, most of the projects in this book are ones I do or have done in class. The best way to see if *Junk Drawer Physics* activities will work for you on a large scale is to try them with your students. Students absolutely love hands-on science. Your most difficult students usually become engaged when asked to do something with their hands. I have included several lab write-ups for these projects at www.junkdrawerscience.com.

Many of these activities are short and can be great for the middle of a lesson. Today's students are bombarded with information all the time, and as a result they have developed shorter attention spans. Using a hands-on activity to break a lesson up is valuable. After the hands-on activity, the students will be settled down and will usually behave better. The best discipline plan is a fun and engaging lesson.

Once you try and love a *Junk Drawer Physics* activity with your students, you can place all the supplies in a shoe box. Label the box with the activity name and it will be ready to go in the future. Scissors, tape, and glue should be in a central location where you can always get to them.

Most successful people had a teacher that believed in them and pointed them in the right direction. This book is valuable to today's teacher because you can get supplies for free. Most business owners would love to help out their local schools if asked. So ask! Go to the fast food restaurant closest to your school and ask the manager if you could have a box of straws. I have never bought straws and I use them for probably 10 labs a year. A glass shop will have scrap mirror and will be glad to cut it for you. Just wrap the edges with duct tape and you have small mirrors for labs. If you are nervous about asking for supplies in person, write a letter.

Most business owners want their local schools to be the best possible, and they will reward you with stuff if you ask. If you develop a bond with a business owner, it may lead to larger items later. I have found it is easier to get lab materials from business owners than it is to get money. They believe in a quality education.

When you find a great activity in *Junk Drawer Physics*, ask your students to save the needed materials. Jars, toilet paper tubes, and the like are present in all houses. Most students would love to bring them in, especially after they see the neat things you do with them.

I teach high school physics, and all of my colleagues and some of my students bring in their broken electronics, vacuum cleaners, and stereo equipment. I cut off the power cords first for safety. About once a semester, we have a deconstruction day. Students love taking things apart. Walk around and tell them if you looking for any items, such as speakers or mini LED lights. Speakers are a great source for magnets and copper wire. Computers are great for small motors and fans. The individual motors and fans will usually run off 9-volt batteries once they are out of the computer. Be sure to recycle all the e-waste when you are finished.

Lastly, never throw out anything that looks like it might have a use in the future. If it looks cool, throw it in the junk drawer. If drawer space is limited, put a plastic box under your bed and toss in all the supplies for future *Junk Drawer Physics* activities.

Glossary

accelerate/acceleration: slowing down or speeding up of an object caused by unbalanced forces

air resistance: friction from hitting either a gas or liquid as an object moves through it (also called drag or drag force)

buoyancy/buoyant: upward force created by a liquid (or gas) that has been displaced

centripetal force: center-seeking force

concave mirror or lens: mirror or lens that is "caved" inward in the middle

density: how tightly packed an object's mass is

elastic: the tendency of an object to return to its original shape when stretched or compressed

electron(s): a negatively charged particle; electrons revolve around the nucleus of each atom and are responsible for electricity

elements: the natural building blocks of matter

energy: the ability to cause an object to move or change shape

focal point: the point where a lens (or mirror) focuses light

free fall: an object falling only under gravity and air resistance

friction: force that opposes motion when two substances rub each other

gravity: force that pulls all objects in the universe toward each other

inertia: property of an object that causes it to resist a change in motion

kinetic energy: action energy

longitudinal (compressional) wave: the type of wave in which the particles vibrate back and forth in the same direction the wave is moving (ex: sound is a longitudinal wave)

mass: the amount of matter in an object

molecule: combination of two or more elements

momentum: measure of how hard it is to slow down or stop an object

neodymium magnets: super strong man-made magnets

neutron(s): a neutral (uncharged) particle; neutrons are found in the nucleus (center) of an atom

nucleation points: small area around which crystals or bubbles can form as a material changes states (solid to liquid or liquid to gas)

perpendicular: exactly 90 degrees from a surface, like the two lines of a T

potential energy: stored energy

proton(s): a positively charged particle; protons are found in the nucleus of an atom

radius: half the distance across a circle

repel: to push away from something else

resonance: vibration at the natural frequency of an object

silicon: natural element that is found in most sand and rocks, and makes up about 25% of the Earth's crust

stalagmite: a tapering column of rock that grows upward from a cave floor

static electricity: buildup or loss of electrons on an insulating material (ex: plastic)

transverse wave: type of wave in which the matter vibrates at 90 degrees to the direction of energy movement (ex: a water wave)

ultraviolet light (UV light): harmful type of light energy that causes sunburns

viscous: thick or sticky fluids that do not flow easily (ex: ketchup)

Also available from Chicago Review Press

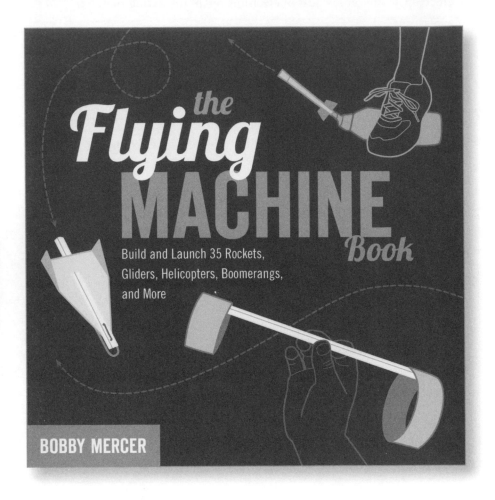

The Flying Machine Book
Build and Launch 35 Rockets, Gliders, Helicopters, Boomerangs, and More
by Bobby Mercer

200 B/W Photos
20 B/W Illustrations

"Hands-on activities that encourage imaginations to soar." —*Kirkus Reviews*

Trade Paper, 208 Pages
ISBN-13: 978-1-61374-086-6
$14.95 (CAN $16.95)
Ages 9 and up

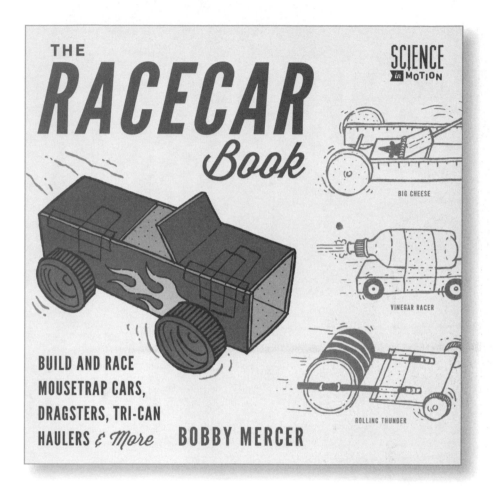

The Racecar Book
Build and Race Mousetrap Cars, Dragsters, Tri-Can Haulers & More
by Bobby Mercer

200 B/W Photos
20 B/W Illustrations

"Highly recommended." —*The Midwest Book Review*

Trade Paper, 216 Pages
ISBN-13: 978-1-61374-714-8
$14.95 (CAN $16.95)
Ages 9 and up

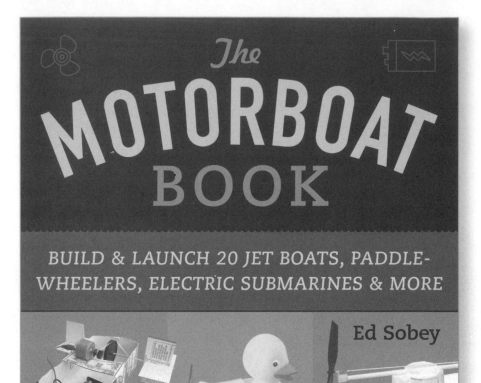

The Motorboat Book
Build & Launch 20 Jet Boats, Paddle-Wheelers, Electric Submarines & More
by Ed Sobey

200 B/W Photos

"These projects will attract those that need to keep their hands moving, as well as teachers who might well tie boat making to social studies projects, or to science/engineering projects."—*Children's Literature*

Trade Paper, 224 Pages
ISBN-13: 978-1-61374-447-5
$14.95 (CAN $16.95)
Ages 9 and up

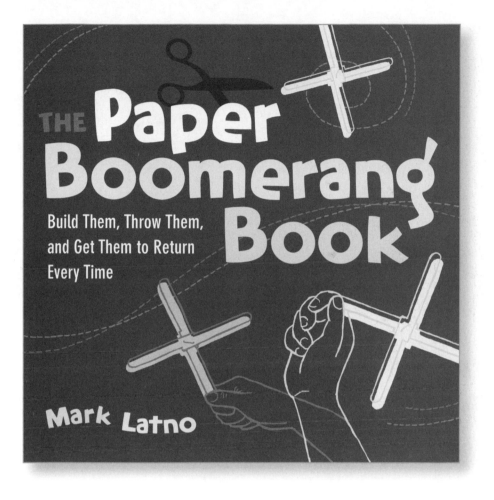

The Paper Boomerang Book
Build Them, Throw Them, and Get Them to Return Every Time
by Mark Latno

90 B/W Photos
30 B/W Illustrations

"This light but earnestly informative how-to guide builds readers into boomerang aficionados by making them first into creators capable of building boomerangs of their own."—*VOYA*

Trade Paper, 160 Pages
ISBN-13: 978-1-56976-282-0
$12.95 (CAN $13.95)
Ages 9 and up

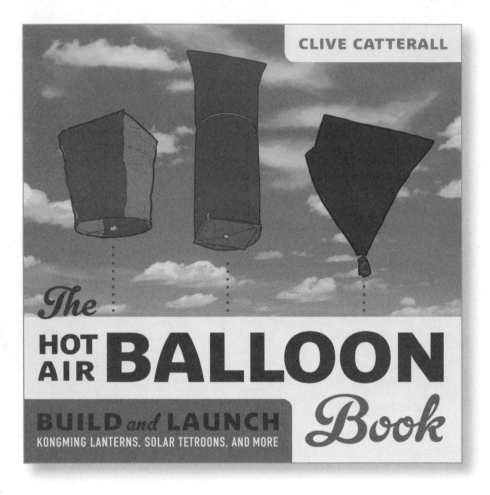

The Hot Air Balloon Book
Build and Launch Kongming Lanterns, Solar Tetroons, and More
by Clive Catterall

400 B/W Illustrations

"This book can make science and learning come alive." —*National Science
Teachers Association*

Trade Paper, 240 Pages
ISBN-13: 978-1-61374-096-5
$14.95 (CAN $16.95)
Ages 9 and up